The Alchemy of Your Life

A Workbook

The Alchemy of Your Life

Discovering the Story & Pattern of Your Life

A Workbook

A. MARINA AGUILAR

In memory of Lorraine "Julia" Geiger,
beloved friend & soror mystica

Table of Contents

MORE TOOLS FOR SELF AWARENESS

Why this workbook and what is Alchemy?

Your life is precious. Within your unique journey there lies deep meaning to be excavated. This workbook is not meant as a memoir, though it could assist you in writing one. *The Alchemy of Your Life* is written from a psychological and spiritual perspective. If you are a materialist, this probably isn't for you. If you are new ager who would rather stay in a "feel good" state all the time, it isn't for you either. But if you have a spiritual perspective and want to do the work of living into the best version of you that you can be, this workbook can help. Spirituality needs psychology, just as much as psychology needs spirituality. If psychological debris is in the way, there is not much room for light. Aldous Huxley, in his book, *The Doors of Perception*, was right when he wrote, "If the doors of perception were cleansed everything would appear to man as it is, infinite." This workbook helps to have a clearer view inside, as well as out into the world.

This project was inspired by my dearest friend of thirty years, beautiful Lorraine Geiger. Her passing in 2021 took me down the death road, bringing to the surface the deeper questions of why we are here and what matters. How it feels when that time comes very much depends on how we have lived. Since 2020, many have taken the opportunity to question and change their lives: where and how they live and what they do for a living, as well as relationships. The pandemic, which put us all indoors, also gave us the opportunity to turn inward and "clean house." Covid changed the world, and it changed our lives.

In my late twenties I discovered (or was I guided to?) what was then an innovative graduate program in psychology offered at Pacifica Graduate Institute in Santa Barbara, California. In fact, this is where I met Lorraine. We were young students learning from those who are now inspiring legends in the field, including Marion Woodman, James Hillman, Robert Johnson, Lionel Corbett, Ginette Paris, Chris Downing, etc....too many to name here.

While traditional programs were mostly oriented toward diagnostics and treatment to improve social functioning, depth therapy, as the name implies, takes a deeper dive into motivation and human potential. Valuing the imagination as the creative force that it is, as well as intuition as a valuable way of perceiving, the depth perspective is not ashamed or afraid to consider the spiritual aspect of the human psyche. In depth work, the sacred is alive and well. Respecting this approach, this workbook approaches your life as a sacred work of art, much as the genuine alchemists approached their experiments.

Why and what *is* alchemy? The father of depth psychology, the Swiss psychiatrist Carl Jung, was surprised to discover alchemical themes in the dreams of his clients. This led him to devote the second half of his life to the study of what, in a rational age, had been considered arcane, cryptic, of little sense or use. Widely viewed solely as a forerunner to chemistry and nothing more, the discovery of alchemy's deeper significance was revolutionary. Jung was the first in a rational age to recognize that alchemy provided a symbolic framework for the evolution of the individual both psychologically and spiritually. He realized that alchemy illustrated through metaphor what is transpiring in the human psyche as we process the events in our lives and evolve.

It is vital to understand that the modern split between the physical and spirit, the rational and the intuitive, did not exist in earlier times. What one did in the material world was understood to have its spiritual implications. Matter was considered one side of the mirror and spirit lay on the other; the two were indivisible.

The alchemist's physical labor involved material elements, but they were never viewed as dead matter. The metals, for example, were associated with cosmic and spiritual forces, and what occurred between them through the manipulation by the alchemist and 'spirit" not only created physical change but also a change in the alchemist him—or herself. Yes, there were female alchemists too, and often a male alchemist had a "soror mystica," a feminine partner, to assist in the work. One of the most famous alchemists was Maria Prophetissa, who lived between the first and third centuries CE in Alexandria, Egypt.

Creative artist and author Kim Krans, in her *The Wild Unknown Alchemy Guidebook,* defines the alchemist of yesterday and today:

> An Alchemist is one who engages with the processes, operations, and materials of the soul. They are an artisan of the elements. To begin this process, all that is required is attention—a willingness

to step into the Laboratory and observe what is there. Soon, with practice and consistency, our observations take on a quality of awe. This happens naturally. We become grateful for the ingredients and materials of our life, even when they are less than ideal. Once reverence enters the Laboratory, it propels the Alchemist into new dimensions. They begin to participate, to experiment with the ingredients in unexpected ways particular to the individual. New gifts and discoveries are revealed.

You, as the alchemist, are invited to that quality of awe as you enter the laboratory. This workbook is offered as that laboratory in which to discover and work with the elements as they have shown up uniquely in your story and on your journey.

The alchemist's work has a goal. It is described variously in metaphor as "turning lead into gold," creating "the Philosopher's Elixir," and creating "the Philosopher's Stone" (i.e., the radiant gem or jewel that is possible through the polishing efforts by the alchemist). However, it's important to point out that the work is not a linear process, but a circular or, better yet, a spiraled one. We meet the same themes many times in life and hopefully, eventually, at a more mature juncture in our process.

Who is this workbook for?

This book is for anyone dedicated to living a conscious life. There is no more important project than deeply considering your unique life story and finding purpose in it. We do this not only for ourselves but for our community and greater humanity.

Every new year, there are multiple offerings to review and consider the trajectory of the past year and to create a vision for the new one coming. This workbook is a greatly extended and deeper dive into this intention. It is *not* intended as a catalogue of outer achievements or failures. It is meant to address the *inner* journey as lived through the outer life. You are born into a set of circumstances and from in utero on, you are collecting experiences. Though we seem to follow a straight line of development, themes reiterate as we make the journey into and through adulthood. Life continuously offers elements to be worked with, a unique chemistry. Your opportunity is to make "gold" of these elements, through separating, purifying, and recombining the effects of your experiences. Through trial and error, you work at achieving value and meaning. There are failures, retries, and successes. Our successes encourage our progress, and what appears to be a mistake, in fact, offers the greatest opportunity to grow and to make a breakthrough. All are experiments that have offered opportunities and gifts, helping us to learn and expand.

You are the alchemist of your life. The journey you are about to take will help you to make sense of what may have seemed to be random experiences of joy and suffering. You are invited to note patterns and appreciate the often-astonishing weaving of events and relationships. Witness how you have learned, changed, and grown. While at times you may have felt life's victim, finding meaning and purpose in the suffering makes you the master of your own alchemical project. It is my dearest wish that this workbook will act as a map and guide to assist you in accomplishing the Great Work of a life well lived.

Introduction

Life seems to just happen with random moments of choice as well as a seeming fate steering its direction. Some lives seem more choice driven and some more fated. But from either perspective, a conscious life includes the ability to look at the major events and relationships in our lives and consider their effects on who we are and who we become, what we have gained and what we have moved on from. And in terms of the heart, who and what have we loved?

The Individuation Project and Alchemy

Depth psychology places a strong emphasis on our individual evolution and the search for meaning in life, but it is important to understand that this emphasis does not exclude our participation with and contribution to others. Our story is inextricably part of and contributes to the greater human story.

A key concept in Jung's theories of personality development is *individuation*. *Individuation* is not ego-centeredness. Ego-centeredness is more of an adaptation to, and differentiation from, the world in which we find ourselves. *Individuation*, on the other hand, is the lifelong process of becoming uniquely you, while paradoxically realizing you are, at the same time, a part of the greater whole of humanity. It is not about superiority or inferiority. The goal of *Iindividuation* is "wholeness," a sense of core strength and balance, transcending social circumstance. The experience is one of having achieved an inner state of coherence and inner peace, having actualized to a greater extent the potentials latent within when you were born.

Spiritual alchemy deeply influenced analytical psychology's founder, Carl Jung, and is a powerful metaphor and path toward understanding the transformational process leading to the possibility of *individuation*. In ancient and medieval history, in both the East and the West, alchemy, the discipline of working with raw elements to create something enduring and precious, was a revered science and art. It is important to note that prior to our modern era, spirit was never divided from matter, so the goal of creating gold from lead meant not only the effort to transmute the physical substance, but also, for the true alchemist, the simultaneous evolution of the personality and soul.

The Alchemical Stages

Alchemy, with its stages and processes, illustrates symbolically the circulating path of growing consciousness. It is not a linear process but a spiral evolution involving retracing our steps at progressive levels of understanding and integration. "Solve et Ccoagula" means dissolve and resolve into a more refined expression; in this case, our perceptions and understanding. This process happens time and time again throughout our lives. What has become hardened in us must eventually soften and dissolve for consciousness to renew and evolve.

The same material in the psyche is metaphorically cooked, dissolved, resolidified, and sublimated time and again as we enlarge our state of awareness, creating a working relationship between the ego and what Jung called the *Self* (capital S). The *Self* is the transpersonal expression of our fullest potential. Unlike the ego, it is the larger truth of our being. One way to imagine this is the potential for the full grown oak tree in the tiny seed.

We begin with our raw experience and psychological reflexes, the *prima materia* in alchemical language, of our lives. Gradually, as we become more conscious, we start to reflect and not simply react, taking greater responsibility for our experience. As we grow in consciousness, we retrieve what is useful and discard what no longer serves. We digest and integrate our experiences and become more whole. Our ego becomes in service to the larger *Self*, and not the master.

Alchemy describes metaphorically this process of personal and collective evolution. Typically, alchemy is divided into four phases: the *Nigredo* (the blackening), the *Albedo* (the whitening), the *Citrinitas* (the yellowing), and the *Rubedo* (the reddening) stages, plus seven substages. The alchemical goal of a life that honors consciousness and values evolution is the Rubedo. Just to note, in medieval heraldry, gold is attributed to the color red (a result of ancient impurities in the smelting process that caused gold to appear reddish in color).

The first, blackening phase, or *Nigredo*, is experienced as a dying-off process accompanied often by a sense of listlessness. The ego experiences a mortification, often through having experienced a humiliation or an upwelling of depression. It can be experienced as what the mystics have called "The Dark Night of the Soul." This is eventually followed by the whitening phase, the *Albedo*, in which we feel a reemergence into life accompanied by a more detached or transcendent perspective. Then, if we continue the work, comes the yellowing phase. During the *Citrinitas*, we purge the old self and ready ourselves for a new level of being. We are in an anticipatory period awaiting the next unfoldment.

Finally, if we are successful, we reach the *Rubedo*, the red phase. This is accomplished through our dedication to the work of consciousness and completed by what the alchemists called "grace." Grace is the invisible spiritual confirmation and a blessing on our efforts. Grace comes in its own time and never through the ego's willing it. The alchemist's job is dedication and devotion to the work. When we feel a new sense of wholeness, it is usually the result of our effort in conjunction with timing, and grace has its own timing.

Though various alchemists have arrived at different numbering of the substages, seven are more commonly agreed upon. However, how they show up in life can be in a different order than the linear one presented here. Sometimes we retrace earlier stages to get a more advanced understanding. Jungian analyst Jeffrey Kiehl outlines the stages in the following order.

Calcinatio—Burning—The Fire

In childhood, we live in the world of psychic *prima materia*, the primary elements of our experience. Until consciousness is brought to bear, the residue of our experiences lies in our shadow. During *calcinatio*, the calcination, or "burning away" process, we consciously confront the *prima materia*, the unworked, unrefined stuff of psyche. We begin to burn off what no longer serves us. Our preconceived notions of our identity and beliefs are tested. Often, we begin *calcinatio* in adolescence, though we may get stuck without much progress for many years. In this workbook, you will find exercises to help you question and rewrite those earlier notions of identity.

Calcinatio, with its *mortificatio* (dying off) element, is a death process for the ego. Some images associated with this experience include fire, black ravens, salamanders, skulls, cemeteries, torture, fevers, sweat lodges, being lost in a desert, or being eaten alive (the ego, as king of the psyche, must die for a more enlightened evolution).

Solutio—Dissolution—The Water

Next comes the dissolution stage. Our former identity and beliefs have been burned away. We no longer feel solid psychologically or spiritually. We are in a state of "letting go." Images of this phase include baths, baptism, floods, pools, tears, and water in general, and we may encounter them in our night and daydreams while traversing this phase. But we do not stay in this watery state. The airier aspect of our consciousness hopefully steps in to dry us out psychically and helps us to create a new order.

Separatio—Separation—The Air

The airy experience of *separatio* helps us to discern and discriminate. At this point, we need to create a new order using mental clarity. We come to understand what is ours, authentically, and what is not. We are sorting things out. In its best expression, we mobilize a healthy ego, rather than an inflated ego, to establish healthy boundaries and make good choices.

At the more advanced level of *separatio,* we cultivate an inner witness. We can view ourselves and our situation from a detached perspective. *Separatio* is often symbolized by knives, swords, scissors, hatchets, and sifters, and anything that reorganizes old structures.

Coniunctio—The Wedding

There are two *coniunctios* in the process of alchemy. In the first, the focus is on attaining a more transcendent and discerning perspective. The first *coniunctio,* seen as a spiritual state, was the final goal from a Christian perspective. But from the more tantric view of alchemy, the operations are not complete until consciousness returns to commune with the physical world of body and nature. The second *coniunctio* will occur after the following processes of *fermentatio* and *sublimatio.* The second *coniunctio* is called *coagulatio* or coagulation, a process of becoming solid again, but in a new form. It is the return to earth, to the grounding of what we have learned and how we have transformed.

Images of the *coniunctio* include sexual union and marriage. We will find these images repeated in the later *coniunctio* of *coagulatio.*

Fermentatio—Fermentation

This is an interim stage associated with the *citrinitas,* or yellowing phase. What is left of the less-refined ego goes through a second death process called putrefaction. Images associated with this phase include rotting and decomposition.

Meanwhile, spirit is being reintroduced into matter, just as fruit juice becomes spirited in the fermentation process. Images of lightening or the descent of birds, as well as of a farmer sowing gold coins into a field, were representations of this stage. We begin "to ground" our new consciousness. Dennis William Hauck, in his classic, *The Emerald Tablet,* has likened the *fermentatio* to the yeasting of dough, allowing the bread to rise. The alchemist patiently waits through the yeasting, or "enspiriting," process.

Sublimatio—Sublimation—The Air

This process serves to yet further purify, refine, and clarify. There is a repetitive process of separation and reintegration of elements in the psyche. We are becoming a renewed, more fully alive human being with a clearer perspective and a mobilized will. A few images associated with distillation include baptismal fonts, the lotus, rainbows, doves, and the eightfold pattern.[1]

Coagulatio—The Second Wedding—Spirit Marries Matter

In this second *coniunctio* and final stage, the old order has entirely passed away, and a new psychological stance and orientation becomes solidified in our experience. Taking actions to establish a new order helps ground this new sense of self. There is a felt sense of rebirth and a "coming down to earth" of one's ideas, ideals, and self.

The preeminent image of this stage is the phoenix rising from the ashes. It is the achievement of the goal of the "alchemical wedding." Circles, and babies too, are

---

1. Dennis William Hauck, *The Emerald Tablet, Alchemy for Personal Transformation.* Just a few in his list of related symbols to the alchemical stages are offered here.

symbols of a newly emerging wholeness. Internal opposites are fully purified and united in a harmonious complementarity within. The ego is now a clearer channel for the *Self*. There will likely be times to come of confusion and repeated cycling through the stages, but something significant has changed and has solidified within. There is no going back to the earlier experiences of an untethered and more vaguely formed sense of self and overreliance on the ego's defenses.

This goal is achieved by a conscious navigation of the repeated cycles of creation and dissolution throughout our lives. Again and again, we create, let go, and then create again as we grow, evolving psychologically and spiritually. We experience the alchemical stages time after time, hopefully at more elevated rungs on the spiral of life.

While you progress through this workbook, you will be invited to notice what you have done with the rough ingredients of "nurture and nature" (your inheritance at birth). Notice what you are still working on. Notice, too, how you have very likely evolved beyond your parents' experience and adaptation to life. Notice how your experiences have deepened you, creating greater wisdom, empathy, and respect for yourself and others. We cycle through these stages and processes. Individuation, like enlightenment, is an ongoing process ever evolving us.

The Spiral of Life and Creation

Human life is a paradox constantly asking us to balance polarities. Recognizing the pattern of paradox and the repeating cycles, like the Taoists of the East, the ancient alchemists considered "the book of nature" as the greatest wisdom teacher. They noted that nature continually expresses herself through a series of births, blossoming, deaths, and rebirths. They applied this observation to their efforts at transmutation, both with physical substances and transmutation's accompanying spiritual journey. They noted this ever-repeating cycle offers repeated opportunities to balance the polarities and arrive at new, more refined expressions.

We are born from the coming together of opposites—male and female. We have right and left sides to our bodies and right and left hemispheres of our brain. Day follows night, activity is restored through sleep, spring and summer are followed by autumn and winter. The wheel turns again, spiraling toward the future, ever repeating in new and often more complex expressions. This is nature's way and is also true for us in our individual lives.

We Descend to Ascend

In the ancient mystery traditions around the world, the journey from life to death was never imagined as an end in oblivion but in a cyclical or spiral return to life in a spiritual and, in many traditions, physical rebirth. Labyrinths and spirals found in archaic and prehistoric stone circles, pictographs, and petroglyphs worldwide symbolized the passage from womb to tomb to rebirth, whether that rebirth was thought to occur spiritually into the cosmos or into another body. Labyrinths and spirals weave us in and out of an ever-recurring pattern. This process is not limited to physical death. Here is a profound psychic reality: we inevitably face transitions *within* life itself. There are many moments, large and small, in which we experience a dissolution of the old way in order to birth the new, perhaps having the added benefit of preparing us for the ultimate surrender.

Though a more overtly feminine understanding of womb/tomb/womb went underground when a patriarchal focus became the norm, the symbolism was carried forward. In the ancient past, the return to the Great Mother was imagined as a return and release, demonstrated by the corpses from the Stone Age found buried in fetal positions in Mother Earth. But as we became more alienated from nature, the passage began to be seen as treacherous and needing the protection of amulets and spells. The body and its processes, and the natural release at death, became feared and in need of control. The "demons" that might be encountered after death, and from which people sought protection, may in fact be quite real as psychic products of that alienation along with repression of our fearful emotions and thoughts. In every case, this is the result of pushing our uncomfortable feelings into the shadow of the unconscious. This brings us to the need for "shadow work."

Shadow Work

While common culture religiously and politically demonized the Dark, the more esoteric shamanic traditions and mystery schools the world over gave people access to this journey into darkness while still embodied, with the intention of integration and renewal. Descent always comes before the ascent. The descent is present in Christianity with the belief that Jesus descended into hell after his crucifixion and before his resurrection. And there are countless myths and fairytales that illustrate the needed passage into the dark before achieving greater light. The descent is into the nether regions of the psyche, to that which we assiduously, though often quite unconsciously, avoid owning in our natures. This is what Jung described as "shadow work." Shadow work does not only consist of examining what we push aside out of pain, guilt, or shame.

It also includes many of our best qualities and talents, which we may have disowned out of misplaced humility and fear. In the world in which most of us have been raised, we have been encouraged either to demonstrate false pride or conversely, false humility, a fear of owning our unique greatness. False humility results in giving our authentic power away to religious, political, or any other elitist authority, usually male in a patriarchal world. It serves all structures of domination.

Without the courage to look honestly into the darker recesses of our psyche, our efforts to resolve pain too often involve what psychologist John Welwood termed "spiritual bypass." "Spiritual bypassing" is defined as a "tendency to use spiritual ideas and practices to sidestep or avoid facing unresolved emotional issues, psychological wounds, and unfinished developmental tasks."[2] One of the purposes of this workbook is to help you bring to consciousness the light, the dark, and the many colors in your life experiences. If you are going to fully claim your journey, your value, your authority, and your complexity, it's important to look into the "closets" and the "basement."

The Invitation

You are invited to create a unique recipe from what is given at birth, finding meaning and your own personal contribution to human life and expression. Our inheritances are the sweet and sour ingredients, the polarities, we received at the start of our journey. These ingredients remain as we enter adulthood. They reappear in our experience at the workplace and in our personal lives. Though we believe we have liberated ourselves from childhood, most often we eventually meet once again the similar dynamics in our relationships with coworkers, authority figures, friendships, and in our intimate connections. If we don't actually meet people like our parents, we still find ourselves reacting to these new experiences with old coping mechanisms that seem to magically create the same pain, the same alienation.

We might wonder why we aren't recreating more joy and security from our early experiences. The reason is that for most of remembered history, a skewed patriarchal history, which has been out of balance and damaging everyone

2. Fossella, Tina (Spring 2011). "Human Nature, Buddha Nature: An Interview with John Welwood" (PDF). *Tricycle:The Buddhist Review*. 20(3)

regardless of gender, our childhood experiences have been a great deal less than idyllic. Still, these experiences have created "the rub" that can wake us up to consciousness and growth. Like the cook in the kitchen tasting a meal that could use a new expression to be tasty, we are offered the opportunity in this life to make something nourishing and perhaps even a unique work of art.

Gnothi Seauton, Know Thyself

This is one of the three aphorisms on the Temple of Apollo at Delphi. The other two are "Nothing to Excess" and "Certainty Brings Insanity." Such wisdom! Self-knowledge, balance, and flexibility are values that express the best of us, and they are hard won. They require consciousness and a real and courageous effort of sorting through personal history.

The meaning of "Know Thyself" has been argued. But for the sake of this workbook, it is meant as the continuing journey of understanding oneself as honestly as possible, even as we continue to grow and change. This understanding relies a great deal on the trajectory of one's *personal* story, including both light and shadow aspects.

The difficulty of a particular background doesn't guarantee the end result. Some well-known examples of triumph over adversity are Viktor Frankl, Mahatma Ghandi, Mother Theresa, Nelson Mandela, and Rosa Parks. These are souls who confronted incredible hardship, becoming real life heroes and heroines, emanating strength and compassion against seemingly impossible odds. Nor does the ease of a background guarantee success! There are endless examples of privilege that have produced shallow and petty people, abusers, tyrants and "ne'er-do-wells."

Your story is precious and unique! Even if you grew up with siblings within the same personal and historical frame of reference, they will likely not view your parents, or one another, just as you do. Each person's experience is their own. Just as you have a unique fingerprint, so too, is your story unique.

What I have discovered in nearly forty years of therapeutic practice and individual psychological and spiritual work is that our lives, our stories, are very much an expression of nature, more a spiral than linear form. We revisit time and again the same basic elements of the story given to us at birth and as we were growing up. With each return comes renewed opportunity to work with those primary elements in different ways, until we break free of whatever restriction was inherent in the pattern, creating a more artful and beautiful expression from our experiences. The movie *Groundhog Day* (1993) is a classic because it expresses, through metaphor and with humor, the truth of this archetypal situation. The lead character relives the same day over and over, choosing different approaches to what confronts him, until he finally finds his heart in relationship to the rest of the town. A new day dawns. The pattern falls away. Until we wake up to the pattern, and find our heart in the solution, it will repeat.

How to Approach This Workbook

You can begin this workbook at any time and review and amend your answers as needed.

Please don't feel pressured to rush. And please don't feel you need to answer every question. *Everything is optional. This is* your *journey.* Only you know the right pace for you. Do one section at a time and give yourself enough space to process the journey on a conscious and subconscious level.

As you work through the questions, especially if you are finding the memories are difficult, take a break. It's important to give yourself time to digest and integrate. If you are mostly a mental person, allow yourself to feel. Drop into your tender heart without judgment either of yourself or of others. We rarely simply allow ourselves to feel, without analysis or blame. The wide palette of our feelings is one of the gifts of being human and a sign that we are fully alive. What is important to realize is that we won't stay in any mood forever. If we allow feelings to move through us, they do move on. If we resist them, they push and pull us from the unconscious.

If you are at an earlier stage than the elder years, just go as far as you can with answering the questions. But even if you are far from the elder stage, it is valuable to read that section and consider the end-of-life questions. It is rather like looking at a map of your final destination on a journey. It helps a great deal to know the terrain in advance. In every enduring spiritual tradition, facing death is a part of the journey to wholeness. Death gives us the impetus to create something of value now. To contemplate how you want to feel when it is time to leave this life can be a strong beacon forward. Living with an underlying, even unconscious, fear of death erodes our ability to live here and now, in a grounded, vibrant presence.

While this is a workbook, and the material can feel heavy, it might also be experienced as a "play book," revealing you to you. It can be a lot of fun to reach the "aha moments" that emerge, as well as a realization of meaning and deeper purpose, and the accompanying exhilaration of a job well done. This workbook is not intended to re-traumatize but ultimately to liberate you. True freedom is *inner* freedom, and the road there is self-knowledge, meaning, and purpose.

Scattered throughout are considerations of the different life stages and tools to help you understand family systems, shadow work, the importance of place, our relationship to nature and our pets, and the importance of intuition and our dreams.

Each part includes a consideration of themes and patterns. Themes are the underlying message or central ideas you notice in each section. Some examples of themes:

· Abandonment

· Overcoming Adversity

· Alienation

· Betrayal

· Change vs. Tradition

· Chaos vs. Order

· Class Differences

· Courage vs. Cowardice

· Crime and the Underworld

· Darkness and Light

· Life and Death

· Dedication

· Disappointment

· Disillusionment

· Displacement

· Guilt

· Heartbreak

· Heroism

· Loneliness

· Loss

· Loyalty

· Outsider or Outlier in Your Group

· Perseverance

· Poverty

· Power

· Race

· Sacrifice

· Self-Reliance

Your Alchemical Journey

At the end of the sections on childhood, adulthood, and elderhood, you will be writing the story of your alchemical journey. You will begin with the *prima materia,* i.e., "the givens," as you came into this world: your family, your culture, your natural temperament. Through addressing the various questions and themes you will bring forward your gifts and talents, and what you have made of your experiences. You are invited to consider the various alchemical stages and how they have shown up in your life. Remember they can show up in any order and are not necessarily sequential after the initial consideration of your *prima materia.* Writing about your experience from the perspective of the alchemist or artist cultivates the "witness," which is so useful in meditation and mindfulness practice. This exercise develops a more objective and discerning view of your experiences.

The way to approach this workbook is with compassionate curiosity. The questions are not intended to cast blame on others or the self, though certainly from a personal perspective there are, and were, "good guys" and "bad guys," as well as characters with shades in between. This is what makes a human story. There are obstacles put in our way and challenges to either meet or walk from. And neither answer is always right all of the time. How we meet these challenges, or not, is what makes us who we are.

Some of the questions may be redundant. If you have already given a similar answer to an earlier question, no need to repeat. Some questions may not apply— for example, the questions regarding siblings or parenting, if neither have been part of your life. Please consider these questions as if you are a compassionate, wise, and objective researcher. Approach them with a perspective of interest and curiosity. They will reveal the primary ingredients and patterns that have made you, you. They offer, too, the potential for healing old family patterns as well as contributing to your own evolution as a person and as a soul. At the end of the workbook, you will find Tools for Deepening and Methods for Healing. These can be worked with at any time while you proceed through the questions.

Self-Care!

Self-care is vital as you work through this book. As you approach deep conscious inner work, you need to experiment and discover the best ways you can regain any lost equilibrium.

Watch what is occurring in your body, your mood, and your thoughts. Do you feel drained or agitated? Do you need to put the work aside and give yourself mental rest? What are some ways you regain inner balance and peace? For some it's walking in nature, lying on the grass, being in or near water, or practicing balancing exercises like yoga, tai chi, aikido, or other forms of exercise that simply let off steam. Talking to a trusted friend, getting a massage, or even just asking for and getting a hug are good options. Surrounding yourself with beauty, listening to music, reading an uplifting book, wrapping a special blanket around you, holding a hot water bottle, and even lighting incense can shift your mood. Any positive sensory change can work wonders. Films that distract and uplift or watching comedy can also relieve a tired mind and heart. Choose self-loving ways to soothe and distract. There is no one prescription for everyone. You will need to experiment with what works for you.

Buy or make an attractive journal in which to further process whatever comes up. Journaling is a huge part of processing and integrating the material. If you are an artist or dancer, use creative expression to work through the material. Creative process in all forms is a tremendous tool for transformation.

If at any time, you find yourself being overwhelmed, stop! If you need assistance and support, please engage a trained therapist with whom you feel comfortable. Recognizing the need for help is a sign of real maturity and strength.

If you experienced extreme trauma, please do not approach this
workbook without the support of a professional therapist experienced
in working with trauma. And if at any time you feel you need immediate
medical attention, call 911.

Create a Self-Care/Reset List

Create a self-care/reset list with ten items or activities that work for you.

_____

_____

_____

_____

_____

_____

_____

_____

_____

_____

And a final suggestion—design an altar or sacred space dedicated to your healing,
growth, and your wholeness. Choose a table, a shelf, or any purposed space. It
should hold at least a candle. You can add objects that represent special meaning
for you. You might choose to include photos of yourself at different ages. Flowers,
incense, and any special stones and crystals are nice additions. Pictures of anyone
you experience as a guide and guardian, for example, images of angels, saints, and
deities, and "spirit animal" protectors are some possibilities.

Light the candle before each session with this workbook, dedicating the time as sacred, just as the alchemists did in preparation for their labor. When you extinguish the candle, thank the fire for its service in your work of transformation. We know devotion was a common practice from the medieval etchings depicting the alchemist at prayer in the laboratory before beginning or returning to the labor. This work is *your* sacred alchemical labor and devotion. You can also leave your journal on the altar after working with it.

May this offering contribute to your self-worth, the clarity of your purpose, and your heart's peace.

Life itself initiates each of us according to our own peculiar stories. Our stories lead us toward our purpose in this world. Each initiation strips something away and gives us a gift. If we want to meet our full form, we are obligated to give that gift to the world.

— Amanda Yates Barnes, *Initiation*

Part One

Growing Up

The Journey of Consciousness

Knowing ourselves *is* the journey of consciousness. The more expanded our awareness, the greater our participation as artists of our human journey. We enter this world with certain "givens": a time, a place, a cultural zeitgeist, a physical body with its gifts and frailties, and with caregivers with certain temperaments, histories, and wounding. To begin, our primary ingredients are the biological and psychological inheritance we receive from our mother and father, who have come together to begin the formation of our new body. In the case of adoption, their biological imprints and (if epigenetic theory is correct) psychological imprints as well will influence our DNA. The psychological ingredients of our adoptive parents will be added.

And if that is not enough, the personalities of and treatment we receive from siblings, extended family, peers, and community will contribute. A way to imagine this is that we are dropped into a kitchen (an alchemical lab) with a set of ingredients that can be orchestrated to create an amazing unique dish or a cacophony of clashing tastes producing something not quite digestible. Once we wake to this fact, we take mastery over our experience. Things in the outer world may not change, but our experience most definitely will, because we have shifted to response, rather than instinctual reaction. It is up to us if and how we will work with these ingredients to prepare a unique creation and our personal contribution to the larger human story.

Some of these questions may initially cause painful memories to surface. Please note that the intention is not to relive the suffering with nowhere to go. Instead, you are invited to witness the situations and relationships from the perspective of your adult self. You are a discerning detective, looking for clues and patterns, and you are distilling wisdom from the experiences, moving forward with greater compassion for yourself...and ultimately for the human condition. Again, if the questions feel overly triggering, stop and seek collaboration with a trusted and trained therapist.

There is a spiritual perspective that suggests that on a soul (not personality) level we have attracted and even agreed to these "ingredients" because they offer experience and the opportunity to develop wisdom. The idea of "soul contracts" with the people who have most strongly impacted our lives is explored in depth in the work of hypnotherapists Michael Newton and Robert Schwartz. Neil Donald

Walsh's *Conversations with God* also offers a more healing and positive perspective of both positive and painful situations and relationships. Whether you believe our lives are a random genetic experiment or that the soul has had a hand in planning our circumstances prior to birth, may this exploration be useful to you in finding personal meaning.

Prenatal and Infancy

We begin with your mother's pregnancy. Considerable research has confirmed that not only the physical condition of the mother but also her psychological state influences the growing of your new body. Whether your birth was a surprise or planned, desired or not, the emotional climate surrounding your mother offers valuable clues to the feeling of being challenged by or welcomed into this world. Around eighteen weeks, the growing fetus begins to hear sounds generated not only by the mother's body but in the surrounding environment. Beyond physically hearing, the infant also picks up on biological information about the mother's mood through the hormones generated by pleasure, fear, anger, or pain. This information forms the infant's first impressions.

If your mother and father were diligent in creating a peaceful ambience when you were forming your body, then your entrance into the world will give you the most welcoming start. If your mother's pregnancy was, for whatever reason, badly timed or the environment itself was stressful, you very likely picked up the biological signals of those stressors. This is the first scene in this new play that will be your life, with you in the starring role. Here are some questions to help you excavate this early foundation:

What was I told, if anything, about my conception and my biological mother's experience of her pregnancy with me? Was she unduly stressed? Did she take care of herself? Were there any addictions? If I know there was a lack of physical care or emotional peace, how do I imagine it affected me?

_____

_____

_____

_____

_____

How do I imagine this might have influenced my sense of safety?

_____
_____
_____
_____
_____
_____

Were there any miscarriages or infant/child deaths before me? If so, did that impact my parent's feelings about the pregnancy and my arrival? How so?

_____
_____
_____
_____

Where was my mother living (in a home with your father, with family, or on her own), and what were the circumstances at the time of my conception?

_____
_____
_____
_____

What was I told about my parents' relationship at the time? If I have not been told, then what can I guess?

_____
_____
_____
_____

What have I been told about my mother's mood and physical experience during delivery?

_____

_____

_____

_____

You may want to take a few minutes now and journey back in imagination to the time and place, when and where you were being born. We are not looking for the objective facts, but rather what you sense might have occurred for you then. These images and hunches come from your psychological impressions. They are as valuable as any proven facts.

What can I imagine the infant me experienced during my mother's pregnancy?

_____

_____

_____

_____

...and during and after my delivery?

_____

_____

_____

_____

What do I know about my biological father's reaction/response to the news of my mother's pregnancy?

_____

_____

_____

_____

Where was my father when I was being born? Was he allowed to be present? Did he want to be? Have I been told anything about this? Your parents may have different versions of this story. If so, what do you make of that?

_____

_____

_____

_____

What do I imagine his feelings might have been? (His feelings might have been joy, fear, anxiety...and, likely, a mix.) Having a child can feel like a monumental responsibility for which he may not have felt prepared. On the other hand, he may have been wishing for a child and very excited.

_____

_____

_____

_____

Do I have any feelings/thoughts about these circumstances? Do I believe or wonder if they have had any impact on my childhood and on me even now as an adult? If so, how?

_____

_____

_____

_____

Did my parents have a preference of one gender over another? If so, was I the desired gender? Did that preference have any influence on how I was raised? Do I have any feelings about this?

_____

_____

_____

_____

How do I imagine my parents felt when they first saw and held me

_____

_____

_____

_____

If I was circumcised, how do I feel/think about that?

_____

_____

_____

_____

If I had siblings, have I been told anything about their reactions to my mother's pregnancy, my birth, and my homecoming?

_____

_____

_____

_____

Have I been told that my family home was mostly peaceful, or not, when I was an infant? Did the baby-me feel an atmosphere of safety, more or less? What might my infant-self have felt about the world, i.e., "the world is a safe and mostly satisfying place," or "I am mostly helpless, and the outside world is undependable and maybe even a frightening place"?

_____

_____

_____

_____

_____

At any point, if difficult feelings arise, you can choose to forego answering until you feel you are ready. Self-care is primary. Our journey inward is not meant to retraumatize. Instead, this work is a journey to reclaim parts of ourselves and heal past wounds. Only we can entirely be there for ourselves. Know when you need to put this work aside. Having a safe "port," for example a trusted friend or, better yet, a trained therapist, can go a long way in helping us manage to avoid being overwhelmed. Please listen to that part of you and take care of yourself on this journey.

Have I been told anything about how I was as an infant? Did I cry a lot, or have trouble nursing or sleeping? Was I a quiet baby? Etc.

_____

_____

_____

_____

Do I have any thoughts about these reports? Do they reveal anything essential in my personality or about the environment and my parents' knowledge and capacity to manage parenting?

_____

_____

_____

_____

_____

If the reports I have been told about myself have been seemingly negative (for example, that I was "a crier" or "difficult"), can I imagine how these reports might have a positive interpretation, indicating a natural strength and need?

An example might be reframing "willful" or "difficult" as an expression of the potential for "determination" and "strength," and maybe I have a voice that needs to be heard and heeded later in life. Find the positive gifts in little you. You were not a horse to be broken, but rather, a child to be guided to your best potential. The section "New Agreements" offers a valuable tool for transforming any negative beliefs that may have been imprinted in your early years.

_____

_____

_____

_____

Where was I born (at home, in a hospital, etc.)?

_____

_____

In what city or area and in what country was I born?

_____

_____

Consider associations you and others make with the location. As an imaginal exercise, envision why your soul might have chosen that particular location. The following questions might help.

What is that place known for?

_____

_____

Is it possible to imagine a connection between aspects of this place and my own destiny and preferences?

For example, a baby born in a city known for its artistic or educational culture might experience its impact on her development. Maybe the place has proximity to the sea, or the desert, which still has significance as an adult. Even the name of the city might invoke some meaningful associations.

_____

_____

_____

_____

_____

_____

What opportunities did this place and time offer for my growth and self-expression?

The place could represent an ideal, or, on the contrary, you may have had to struggle to overcome what it represents. Perhaps you could not leave but wanted to. In any case, the context affected the direction of your life, at least at the start. Can you find a value in these circumstances?

_____

_____

_____

_____

_____

_____

_____

Naming is important. The sound of a name carries a particular frequency associated with you. If your name has a meaning, that too has significance regarding a description, an ideal, expectations, familial values, and even longing.

What is my full birth name?

_____

_____

How was/were my name(s) chosen? Who chose and why? Was there any controversy in my family about my naming? Did I receive any ancestral names or names of important people to my parents? If so, what was I told about these people?

_____

_____

_____

_____

_____

_____

_____

_____

Do I feel that legacy has impacted me and the hopes/expectations from my family? How so?

_____

_____

_____

_____

_____

Do I like my birth name(s)? Do I feel it/they suit me?

_____

_____

_____

_____

Did I change my name? Or if I want to change my name, what would I choose? Why?

_____

_____

_____

_____

What do I imagine my name(s) say about me? Does it feel accurate? If so, how? If not, why?

_____

_____

_____

_____

Context

In what historical era and place, racial context and generation, etc., was I born?

Examples include being born Black during the Civil Rights movement and Vietnam protests, or during the Cold War as a baby boomer (the immediate generation born following World War II), or as a GenX'er, or a Millennial growing up during the leap into a post-9/11 world dominated by the internet and technological advancement.

_____

_____

_____

_____

What benefits/privileges and challenges/difficulties did this context present?

_____

_____

_____

_____

_____

How did I benefit and/or suffer from the circumstances of my birth? What opportunities for my own growth were stimulated by these circumstances?

_____

_____

_____

_____

_____

What was the political and economic climate like at the time? How might this climate have contributed to my parents' mental and emotional states and possibly affected me as a result?

_____

_____

_____

_____

Were your parents immigrants to the country where you were born? Maybe they were exiles or running from trauma in their home country. This would add another layer of complexity. Were you, as a small child, an immigrant? If so, consider how these circumstances affected the atmosphere at home.

_____

_____

_____

_____

_____

_____

Memories

What are my earliest memories (infancy, toddler years)?

Most often memories of this time are more like snapshots. If any linger, describe them. What do you imagine you might have been feeling at that time? If available, find some baby pictures of yourself and consider the expression on the face and the body language of this little one. What do you remember or imagine this child
is feeling?

_____

_____

_____

_____

_____

_____

_____

_____

If the young child is grieving, confused, or angry, see your adult self going back to the past and comforting her or him. Maybe you see your young one in her room, feeling sad, angry, or lonely. Imagine your adult self entering the room and spending time with the child. Be that child's "guardian angel." Be the reassurance and love she or he needs. Let this young one know you love and will care for them, no matter what. Your inner child is still with you at no matter what age.

What do I remember from the ages three to six, if anything?

Again, these memories tend to be "snapshots," containing some remembered feelings and thoughts.

_____

_____

_____

_____

_____

_____

_____

_____

Who were the most important "others" in my life then?

This list might include people, pets, trees, and even toys and imaginary friends.

_____

_____

_____

_____

_____

_____

_____

_____

What stories, if any, was I was told about my early years, and what was happening in my family? How may have that affected how I felt in my environment?

_____

_____

_____

_____

_____

_____

The home, our family, and our neighborhood are our whole world when we are very young. Here are some questions to consider.

Overall, what did it *feel* like in my home during my early years? What was the emotional temperature? Did it fluctuate a great deal or was it mostly stable? How so? Did my home feel mostly safe or chaotic, unpredictable?

_____

_____

_____

_____

_____

_____

How much time do I remember spending alone and with others?

If you had siblings, maybe alone time was rare. You may have enjoyed a full, warm house. Or maybe you craved "alone time." If you were an only child or a child with some distance in age from your siblings, then you might remember more "alone time." If the family was small, you may have enjoyed playing on your own or you may recall memories of loneliness.

_____

_____

_____

_____

_____

_____

Do you feel your place in the family has had any lasting effect on your perspectives and expectations?

_____

_____

_____

_____

_____

_____

What are my most difficult memories from early childhood?

_____

_____

_____

_____

_____

_____

What are my happiest memories?

_____

_____

_____

_____

_____

_____

Who did I feel loved by and who did I love to be around? Who was especially important to me?

_____

_____

_____

_____

_____

What were my favorite treats?

_____

_____

_____

_____

Do I remember any unusual dreams or experiences? Were they comforting, scary, or neutral?

Examples might include feeling very, very big and alternately very small; hearing nature, toys, or invisible friends speak; hearing music that wasn't playing in the physical world; repetitive dreams or nightmares that had no apparent relationship to the environment; seeing colors around things and people; maybe even seeing what others might call "an alien." I have encountered these examples in the memories of my clients in my nearly forty years of therapeutic practice.

_____

_____

_____

_____

_____

_____

What do you make of these memories now?

_____

_____

_____

_____

_____

_____

_____

Themes

What themes do I detect in my very early experience?

Examples might include a general sense of welcome and acceptance laying a foundation of safety in the world, or conversely, you might spot themes of loss and abandonment and the beginning of challenges to your sense of trust and safety.

Maybe those themes will later play a significant part in evolving you as your life progresses. I personally experienced an early theme of abandonment that ultimately served to grow my independence and autonomy, after many twists, turns, and detours trying to cure abandonment by attaching too quickly to unsuitable partners. How about you?

Revisit the themes list in "How to Approach This Workbook" to help you answer this question.

_____

_____

_____

_____

_____

_____

How did I experience love and affection? Did I experience the fully met, loving gaze of my caregivers? If not, what may I have learned early on about life and how to protect my heart?

There are many reasons your mother, father and caregivers may not have been able to give you this affirmation of love in the "loving gaze." They may have been overwhelmed with stress, worries, and fears. Still, your young self learned from this lack of meeting. What ways did your young self learn to protect the heart? Do these early imprints still carry an impact on your experience of love and safety today? What did you learn about your own worth and emotional safety?

_____

_____

_____

_____

_____

_____

Consider what traits you have alchemized from those earlier years and what remains to be transmuted? Maybe you were a willful and stubborn child or a fearful, anxious one. How have you worked with those qualities? Maybe your _prima materia_ of willfulness and stubbornness has transmuted into discipline and determination. Maybe your _prima materia_ of fearful anxiety has found a balance in healthy caution and self-care.

_____

_____

_____

_____

_____

_____

Regarding difficult memories, have you been able to find greater meaning and purpose in those experiences? Coming to peace with difficult events can take a lifetime or may not even be possible. The question is offered here for your contemplation.

Examples of finding greater purpose might include developing greater empathy, self-expression, or autonomy, or working for peace, better communication, justice, etc. What did the experiences of your early life instill or inspire in you?

_____

_____

_____

_____

_____

Remember to revisit your self-care, reset list as needed. After every session with this material, comfort and treat yourself with something on your list. This journey into the past is brave but challenging work. Honor yourself for what you have experienced and taken on. Appreciate how you have learned and grown.

Loving Your Inner Child

The child within lives in each one of us, even if we are now in adult bodies. The child within is not a physical child as such, but an energetic part of us which is important to our spiritual success and material well-being. It is this part of us that feels and experiences the magic in life. It is this part of us that is open to ideas and inspiration, to learning, and is naturally very curious and adventurous. It is also often the part of us that was taught to fear, to hold back and dampen down our individuality, boldness, and uniqueness.[1]

The inner child is vibrantly alive, sensitive, curious, loving, and playful. But often, in the process of being initiated into our families and culture, we are domesticated through fear and separation. We learn to repress parts of ourselves to fit in, to secure love, and to preserve safety. Inner child work is all about befriending this part of ourselves and often re-parenting it.

Some useful ways to create a good inner parent for your inner child is to not only show this part of yourself understanding and compassion, but also to note when you *do* see good parenting in others. If you meet and witness good parents and parenting, take note of it. But if no living examples are available, you can look for movies and literature that depict a positive parent/child relationship. I grew up with a loving but narcissistic mother, so when I saw the movie *Stella* (the 1990 remake with Bette Midler) the story seemed highly improbable—in fact, impossible. I didn't believe there really were mothers like that. Finally, I did realize that indeed there were and are, and that went a long way to healing the mother inside of me and my inner child.

Write a list of all the traits you can imagine in a good mother and good father in your journal. Name all the traits you wished for and maybe partly did have in your parenting. Metaphorically, you are planting healthy seeds of internal good parents that will grow over time to support you as you need to be supported and loved. Your subconscious will take note of all these messages and now be able to

1. Alana Fairchild, *Crystal Masters 333*, Chapter 3, "Initiation of the Child Within." Pages 61-67.

construct a more expanded view of what is possible for you moving forward. It has been proven that the subconscious believes what we picture. For example. baseball pros often imagine a successful pitch or hit before they act, with gratifying results. Your subconscious believes what you can picture.

Some additional ways to get in touch with this part is to write a dialogue between the adult you and your younger self. Listen without judgment and take seriously your child's answers. Give her or him support and kindness. You can also spend time with photos of little you and consciously give love to this part, especially when you hear her or his sadness and complaints. If you find a happy photo of yourself as a child, call in that joy, sweetness, exuberance, and innocence. Recall and reclaim that part.

If you are remembering hurtful experiences, are you able to notice when you experienced these same feelings later in life? What are your triggers now, triggers that began when you were misunderstood, hurt, or criticized in the past? Are you able to have compassion for why those feelings still come up? Can you offer yourself the love and support your inner child needs now just as she or he needed it then? At some point, those triggers will lose their sting because you have given this part of yourself compassionate permission, attention, and unconditional love.

You can also get in touch with your child by writing a letter from her or him with your non dominant hand. You can respond as the adult with your dominant hand. Though it can be quite challenging to write with the nondominant hand, it serves surprisingly well to bring forward that young, unschooled, and deeply feeling young self.

It takes a lot of courage to decide to be present with and heal your inner child. Mostly we just want whatever pain associated with that time to go away and to get on with living now. But she or he is always there in the background, and many times when we are hurt in life, it goes back to her or his early suffering and sadness. Be present to your inner child without judgment. This is so important. If you are good at visualization, imagine holding your child on your lap, giving all the space, comfort, and support she or he needs. Stay present with the emotions that come up.

And there is more to this than just healing your inner child. She or he not only needs your protection, but your child also needs to have a place to express and play freely without fear and constraint. Some ways you might let her/him express herself/himself are through dance, drumming, running, skipping, painting, exuberant laughter, and unbridled joy.

The child's feelings matter whether they are exuberant, sad, angry, lonely, or fearful. When we are present to those feelings, we allow for a release and inner freedom. We free ourselves from unexpected triggers in the present rooted in deep woundings from the past.

> It is only with genuine compassionate presence that we are able to truly feel and consequently release our feelings and any stories attached to them. As this happens, we can finally move on to create and attract new experiences for ourselves. This feels more alive and empowered than getting caught up in history seeming to repeat itself (such as when we see our father in our employer or our mother in our lover, for example, or hearing our parents' words coming out of our own mouths when trying to parent our own children, despite our best efforts to do things more consciously).[2]

Finding time to allow the free, playful child to just have fun is important. In your journal, consider ways you can let your playful child come out and express herself or himself. This aspect of you is part of your authentic self, full of life and possibility, before you were domesticated.

On the following page, draw or paste photos evoking your life during this time. Even though the years have rolled on and you have matured, there is always a young part within you. Inviting them back into our consciousness, honoring our younger parts, and giving them loving attention are valuable forms of "soul retrieval."

2. Ibid.

Photo Memories

This is me when I was a baby and young child.

If you don't have photos, then choose an image (drawn, or from the internet or a magazine), evoking this period of life. This is intended to help you connect with and honor this part of you and your history.

Middle Years: 7-12

In our middle growing-up years, we are starting to include our peers and other adults we encounter in our neighborhood and at school in our experience. While what is happening at home is still primary, what happens with our peers, teachers, and caregivers (such as babysitters or scout leaders), impacts our experience and sense of self. We will begin by looking at home, starting with mother, then father, stepparents if we had them, then siblings and our extended family. Finally, we will move on to the wider social context.

While no parent is perfect, all we need are "good enough" parents and caregivers to move forward without too much hindrance. Again, these are general questions that serve to bring your attention to the overall impressions that have stayed with you and could influence you today.

What was the availability of parents and caregivers during this time? Did that availability change and, if so, how? How did I feel about that?

_____

_____

_____

_____

_____

_____

Was my mother, in general, a safe and comforting resource when needed? Did I feel loved by her?

_____

_____

_____

_____

Was her parenting consistent enough? How did I experience her consistency, or was her attention highly unpredictable?

_____

_____

_____

_____

_____

_____

Did her accessibility or her lack of presence contribute to or impact my sense of trust, safety, and self?

_____

_____

_____

_____

_____

_____

_____

_____

Did I feel I was important to her? If so, in what way?

_____

_____

_____

_____

Did I feel she was pleased with who I was, or did I feel she wished I were different? Did I feel she *saw* me? If not, how so? Did I feel she was proud of me?

_____

_____

_____

_____

Generally, did I feel her support? Do I recall any instances in which I especially felt her support or lack of it?

_____

_____

_____

_____

Did I feel my mother was proud of me?

_____

_____

_____

_____

_____

Did I feel proud of her or not? Did I basically like the person my mother was or not? How was that for me? How did these feelings affect who and how I wanted to be or not be?

_____

_____

_____

_____

_____

How did I see *myself* as a result?

Examples might include smart/stupid, capable/incapable, strong/weak, likeable and lovable, weird/different, or unwanted.

_____
_____
_____
_____
_____
_____

Has this changed for me as an adult? How?

If not, this will be something to work through and heal. Look at Don Miguel Ruiz's Four Agreements outlined in the New Agreements section later in this chapter (better yet, read his book), for valuable assistance in releasing any lingering harmful beliefs.

_____
_____
_____
_____
_____

Was my father, in general, a safe and comforting resource when needed? Did I feel loved by him?

_____
_____
_____
_____

Was his parenting consistent enough? How did I experience his consistency or lack thereof?

_____

_____

_____

_____

Did his accessibility or his lack of presence contribute to or impact my sense of trust, safety, and self?

_____

_____

_____

_____

_____

_____

_____

Did I feel my father was proud of me?

_____

_____

_____

_____

Did I feel proud of him or not? Did I basically like the person my father was or not? How was that for me? How did these feelings affect who and how I wanted to be or not be?

_____

_____

_____

_____

_____

_____

How did I see *myself* as a result?

Examples might include smart/stupid, capable/incapable, strong/weak, likeable and lovable, weird/different, or unwanted?

_____

_____

_____

_____

_____

_____

Has this changed for me as an adult? How?

If not, this will be something to work through and heal. Look at Don Miguel Ruiz's Four Agreements outlined in the New Agreements section later in this chapter (better yet, read his book), for valuable assistance in releasing any lingering harmful beliefs.

_____

_____

_____

_____

_____

_____

How about stepparents? Did you have them? What were those relationships like?

_____

_____

_____

_____

_____

_____

Grandparents

Did I know my grandparents? Did one or more of my grandparents have an influence on my early life? How so? How did we get along? How important were my grandparents in my life during this time?

_____

_____

_____

_____

_____

_____

What about other caregivers (babysitters, teachers, counselors, etc.)? What impact did they have on you as a child?

_____

_____

_____

_____

_____

_____

New Agreements

In his book *The Four Agreements*, Don Miguel Ruiz points out that when we are young, we are directly or implicitly told information about ourselves and our capabilities by the people around us. Adults have enormous power at this time in our lives because, as children, we trust and believe the "big people." We absorb these judgments, though mainly they stem from the adult's personal situation and beliefs. These assessments are often projections and have little to do with our true value and capabilities. Certainly, any categorical statements about our perceived failings at the time were just that—perceived, but largely inaccurate, as they are shaped by the worldview of our caregivers.

Perhaps you agreed consciously or unconsciously to the criticisms, moods, and personal beliefs of your teachers, parents, other adults, and peers around you. Even an acting out child with disruptive traits can learn to channel those traits in a positive direction. Pathologizing a child is deeply harmful.

What were you told about yourself at such an impressionable age? If you heard negative judgments, consider the possibility of dissolving those disempowering "agreements." Can you imagine a positive expression of whatever fault was found in you then? An example might be having been labeled "stubborn." Stubbornness, when expressed in healthy ways, is indicative of a power that can be directed toward positive accomplishment. Another example is having been labeled "spacey," or ADD. Maybe you were bored and had too little stimulation for your creativity and intelligence. Perhaps you were accused of being "manipulative"? Maybe there seemed to be no other way to be heard. Maybe no one was willing or able to listen in your family?

Since the 1970s, these differences in behavior have often been drugged into compliance. But a wider range of teaching methods and a more positive reframe of what we are observing in children is both possible and necessary.

What negative information, given to me by parents, teachers, and peers, might I have agreed to? What labels did I receive? What labels did I accept? What labels did I reject?

_____

_____

_____

_____

_____

_____

Did my caregivers transfer any of their personal feelings of inadequacy and shame onto me? Did I unconsciously agree to carry that shame?

_____

_____

_____

_____

_____

Would I like to dismantle those unhelpful agreements now?

_____

_____

_____

_____

_____

What new agreements will I make with myself regarding who I am and what my capabilities are moving forward?

_____

_____

_____

_____

_____

Working with Shame

Some of our earliest memories might include feeling shamed. The first story of humanity in the Judeo-Christian Bible recounts Adam and Eve's experience of shame. Shame seems to awaken us to our separation from source, whether that source be our mother, our father, God, or some other influential figure in our early lives. Shame humiliates us and, when chronically experienced, can rob us of our internal dignity, self-worth, and self-trust.

Much work has been done by John Bradshaw on unveiling the wounding of early shame. He teaches that the healing begins with becoming reacquainted with and healing our "inner child." Other researchers in shame have followed Bradshaw's lead, including Brené Brown and David Bedrick.

When we have been shamed, we instinctively avoid vulnerability as a strategy to protect ourselves from further shaming. This defense as a way of life precludes real intimacy in our relationships and the healing that could offer. Brené Brown's work addresses the importance of reclaiming our vulnerability as a courageous act and evidence of our inner strength, while discerning with clarity where and with whom it is safe to be vulnerable. Healthy vulnerability implies healthy boundaries.

David Bedrick describes the shaming process as not only the violation of someone's dignity and worth by a perpetrator, but quite often this shaming is made far worse by a gaslighting witness. That witness might be a mother who allows the father to beat their child, explaining later that they deserved it, or worse, telling them it never happened. A whole culture and religious community can act as the gaslighting silent witness, minimizing the abuse, making excuses for it, and even applauding it (as is evident in the saying, "Spare the rod, spoil the child"), or feigning blindness. Bedrick's work (a process he calls "unshaming") encourages clients to express, through their body, the unexpressed emotions of having been shamed and/or gaslit by witnesses. The therapist, meanwhile, acts as an affirming, compassionate witness, positively re-empowering the client.

Abuse in any form creates emotional and cognitive dissonance in a child. Whereas the body and soul instinctively seek protection, the surrounding environment annihilates personal boundaries and effectively destroys the child's self-respect.

Children who are shamed learn to mistrust their own impressions, desires, and instincts. Very often, this follows the child into adulthood. They no longer trust their internal authority and knowing. This self-mistrust then propels them into a repeated search for "healing" and advice-seeking from others. Reclaiming faith in our own wisdom—knowing what is and isn't personally right for ourselves—is essential in the unshaming process.

Alternatively, the shamed child might go in the opposite direction, becoming an adult bully who uses their power over others, continuing the shaming cycle. Hidden, unaddressed anger at the violations we receive in childhood can turn the victim into a perpetrator for the next generation.

Bedrick's answer in both cases is to offer the sufferer the experience of an affirming witness to their entrenched pain, while guiding the client to get in touch with their healthy instincts of self-protection. By acting as an affirming witness and coach, he returns self-worth, dignity, and personal power to the client.

Denial of personal power as well as the misuse of it are rooted in shame. Finding an affirming, compassionate witness to our suffering, however entrenched, is powerfully healing.

Siblings: My Place in My family

Family Systems

Family Systems Theory delineates the typical roles played by children in the family. Though there are some differences and further elaborations, there are five main strategies children either adopt or are given by the family. These roles show up most strongly in dysfunctional families and/or families in which the caregivers suffer from alcohol abuse. But they can be useful in identifying what roles we might have played as children to a greater or lesser degree in all types of families and home lives.

These roles include the Hero/Heroine (sometimes called the Golden Child), the Scapegoat (or Identified Patient), the Clown (or Mascot), and the Lost Child.

The *Hero/Heroine* is seen as the leader and achiever of the family and puts on a good front. These children tend to focus on perfection and often are academically or athletically successful, hence their favored place as the family's golden child.

The *Scapegoat/Identified Patient* is the troubled child who distracts the family with a persistent need for negative attention. Their distraction, however, serves the family by bringing them together to solve the problems they present, as well as distracting the parents from their own underlying and unaddressed conflicts. The child is, in fact, acting out those conflicts.

The *Clown or Mascot* relieves family tension with humor, silliness, and playful antics. They often use this adaptation in the classroom at school as well.

The *Lost Child* disappears by being quiet or preoccupied in their own world. You can find them lost in a book or in their own imagination. They tend to go under the radar at home and at school.

It has been observed that the middle child will often take on the emotional pain of the parents, but this is not necessarily true in all cases.

If you were close in age to your siblings, then you may be able to spot a more ongoing role you and your siblings took on in your family If you were an only child, or a child separated by at least ten years from your other sibling(s), maybe you see yourself in more than one of these roles as you grew up.

Did I have any brothers or sisters? What was the birth order? Was I an "only," the oldest, a middle, or the youngest child growing up? Did that order change during my childhood. If so, when?

_____

_____

_____

_____

_____

If I had siblings, can I identify them with any of the family roles listed above? What role best suits how I remember my participation in the family

_____

_____

_____

_____

_____

_____

_____

_____

_____

_____

If I had siblings, what was my relationship with each of them when we were children? Who was I closest to and who felt more distant? Did that stay the same or change over the years? If I was an "only," how did I feel about that when I was growing up?

_____

_____

_____

_____

_____

_____

_____

_____

_____

_____

How did each of my siblings treat me, and how did I interpret that treatment as information about myself?

_____

_____

_____

_____

_____

_____

_____

_____

_____

_____

Who could I trust, and who couldn't I trust?

_____

_____

_____

_____

_____

_____

Did my relationship with my siblings influence how I expected to be received by the world outside my home? Did I feel like I needed to prove my family wrong (or even right) about who I was?

_____

_____

_____

_____

_____

_____

From my experience in the family system and the role(s) I played, what did I decide about myself?

_____

_____

_____

_____

_____

_____

An interesting exercise to try with several other participants:

Standing in a line, take your place as whomever you were in the birth order of your family. Feel that position. Next, switch places with each other, feeling the difference of that position in the birth order. Some interesting revelations of the impact of birth order will surface, giving information about both its benefits and liabilities. If you cannot do this physically, at least imagine standing in the other positions.

What did your place in the birth order of your family give to you, and what did it withhold from you? Can you find any positive value that you gained in your own development resulting from your position in the birth order?

_____

_____

_____

_____

_____

_____

_____

_____

_____

My Childhood Environment

Did I live in an urban, suburban, or rural environment growing up? Did this change at any point? If so, how did I feel about that change in my surroundings?

_____

_____

What was my relationship to nature?

_____

_____

_____

_____

Did I have a special place when I wanted or needed to be alone as a child?

_____

_____

_____

_____

Did I have any special toys? What made it/them special?

_____

_____

_____

_____

Did I have favorite stories and favorite pretend games? What were they?

Play often reveals traits and interests inherent to our personality. Play is a rehearsal for grown-up life.

_____

_____

_____

_____

_____

_____

Can I detect any resonance between those special stories and favorite games during childhood and what is important to me in my life now? Is there any resonance to my current work or interests?

Were these games and stories in any way predictive of your life's work/purpose?

_____

_____

_____

_____

_____

_____

Did I have any invisible friends? Who, and how were they important to me?

_____

_____

_____

_____

What are my memories of these "invisible friends?"

_____

_____

_____

_____

When did I stop feeling them near me? What happened? Did I grieve their loss or naturally move on?

_____

_____

_____

_____

Did I experience anything that might ordinarily be termed "supernatural," i.e., an out-of-the-ordinary occurrence?

As described in the section on our earlier years, examples might include seeing a spirit, ghost, or fairy, experiences of feeling very big, then very small, or a sense of distortion of time and space, etc.

_____

_____

_____

_____

_____

_____

Was I able to share any of those unusual experiences with others? If so, with whom did I share it? If I didn't share, why not?

_____

_____

_____

_____

_____

Do I have any strong memories of awe and wonder? What are they?

_____

_____

_____

_____

What was deeply important to me as a child? What was a major interest?

_____

_____

_____

_____

_____

What did I love to do most as a child? What was the most fun to me?

Examples might include riding bikes with friends, playing sports or make-believe, playing "dress up," dancing, singing, etc. If you played make-belive, what were the scenarios? Do you find any clues as to what you later did in life?

_____

_____

_____

_____

_____

_____

What upset me most as a child? How did I handle those feelings? How did I receive comfort? Did I find ways to comfort myself? How?

_____

_____

_____

_____

_____

_____

What about my body? Was it strong and healthy, or did I struggle with any physical issues? Did I experience any surgeries as an infant or child?

_____

_____

_____

_____

_____

_____

Was I accepted and included in sports and/or other physical activities or shunned and laughed at? How did these gifts or struggles impact me?

_____

_____

_____

_____

_____

_____

What do I see as the purpose of schooling in my early years?

_____

_____

_____

_____

_____

_____

What did teachers comment about me? What did/do I make of these comments?

_____

_____

_____

What was easy for me in school? What did I enjoy? Why?

_____

_____

_____

_____

_____

_____

Do I still enjoy it?

_____

Have those initial interests evolved into something I've pursued in my adult life?

_____

_____

_____

_____

_____

Can I think of any talent that may have been suppressed because it was not safe to acknowledge it in my family, at school, or in the larger world?

Maybe an interest in art, music, or acting was discouraged because the family felt it was impractical or there simply was a lack of funds for lessons. Maybe a child's interest and even talent frightens the family. I have heard two examples of a family discouraging a child's writing for fear that the family secrets would be exposed.

_____

_____

_____

_____

_____

What subjects were difficult for me? What did I decide about myself as a result? Do I believe an understanding/supportive teacher or tutor would have made a difference? What did I decide about myself because of those difficulties?

_____

_____

_____

_____

_____

_____

Did I tend to hang out with the smart kids, cool kids, troublemakers, or some other group? What does that friend group tell me about who I was at the time and possibly still am?

For example, if you hung out with troublemakers that could have been a positive sign of independence. If you were a loner, what does that tell you about yourself then and now? Maybe, though your grades were poor, you hung out with the smart kids. That is a clear indicator you were smarter than you knew at the time.

_____

_____

_____

_____

_____

_____

Were there any teachers or mentors I remember positively? Who were they, and why did they have a positive impact on me?

_____

_____

_____

_____

_____

_____

Did I experience any teachers who abused their position either through unjust punishment or any other form of mistreatment?

_____

_____

_____

_____

_____

_____

What affect did that abuse or judgment have on me moving forward? Do I still feel triggers related to these experiences? Am I particularly sensitive to misjudgment, for example? Do I expect judgment or abuse in my relationships?

_____

_____

_____

_____

If so, how have I learned to manage these triggers? What has been my typical response when feeling threatened?

Fight, flight, freeze, or fawn are typical trauma reactions. Do I notice one is more typical for me when my relationships feel stressed?

_____

_____

_____

_____

Do I think I use these defenses appropriately? If I tend to react unconsciously, would I like to become more conscious and possibly moderate those reactions now that I am an adult?

Maybe you jump too quickly to anger? Maybe you retreat too quickly, without letting the other know you will be ready to discuss when things calm down. Or maybe you say anything to pacify the other person. What is your instinctive reaction?

_____

_____

_____

_____

Do I feel my impression of authority was basically healthy, or has it been damaged by my experiences?

_____

_____

_____

_____

_____

_____

Was I a more rebellious, independent, or mostly cooperative child at school?

_____

_____

Did this match my personality as my family knew me, or was I different at school than I was at home? If so, were there any reasons that account for this difference?

Therapeutic theory suggests that acting out in a particular environment can actually indicate a child feels *greater* safety there. A child might act out at home but not at school, or vice versa. This indicates greater trust and safety in the acting out location.

_____

_____

_____

_____

_____

_____

Did I have any best friends in my childhood? Who were they? What made them special?

_____

_____

_____

_____

_____

_____

What did I value in these friends?

_____

_____

_____

_____

_____

_____

Did I have a boyfriend or girlfriend? Do I have any fond or painful memories of them?

_____

_____

_____

_____

Did I learn anything about relationships and myself in those early relationships? If so, what did I learn?

_____

_____

_____

_____

_____

If/when these friendships ended, what do I recall about that time? Was the ending natural, or did it feel like a difficult or maybe even a devastating loss?

_____

_____

_____

_____

_____

_____

_____

Who were the other significant adults who affected my life as a child? How?

Examples might include grandparents, extended family, babysitters, neighbors, religious authorities, etc.

_____

_____

_____

_____

_____

_____

_____

_____

_____

What kind of child was I, what was my temperament in general? Quiet and introverted, or active and extroverted? Did that change situationally or over time?

_____

_____

_____

_____

How did I grow personally and interpersonally through these formative years? Can I find the growth in the difficult experiences as well as in the happier ones?

_____

_____

_____

_____

_____

_____

_____

_____

_____

Memories

What are my most beautiful, happy memories from this time?

_____

_____

_____

_____

_____

How have these happy memories influenced my life moving forward?

_____

_____

_____

_____

_____

_____

_____

What are my most difficult memories from this time?

_____

_____

_____

_____

_____

_____

How did these experiences change me or help me grow?

_____

_____

_____

_____

_____

_____

_____

How have these experiences influenced my life moving forward?

_____

_____

_____

_____

_____

_____

Checking In

If any of these memories are triggering, remember to take care of yourself, using tools from your self-care, reset list. Remember, too, to honor yourself for what you have been through and how these experiences have not only affected you but also how they grew you into who you are today. You are a survivor and maybe even a thriver. Notice how they have impacted the choices you make today. Consider whether you are at peace with how you have worked with these experiences, and whether there are any changes you would like to make. Use your personal journal to process and go deeper.

The Body

How did I generally feel in my body as a child?

Consider the feeling tone of the experience you had of your physical body as a child. Some examples include experiencing your body as strong/vibrant, powerful, agile, awkward/ugly, small or weak, etc. There could be a combination of experiences.

_____

_____

_____

_____

The Heart

What was my heart's experience of these years?

Some examples of how your heart might have felt include open, hopeful, trusting, and joyful; excited, creative, fearful, careful, confused, broken, sad, or helpless. Use these words or your own to describe your general emotional state as a child.

_____

_____

_____

_____

Is there any healing that needs to happen for your inner child's heart? How can you address that?

_____

_____

_____

_____

The Mind

How about my relationship with my mind during childhood? What was the general tenor of my thoughts?

Examples might include excited, stimulated, creative, depressed, scared, etc. Again, aim for general descriptions, as there are always good and bad moments and shades in between.

_____

_____

_____

_____

The Spirit

On a spiritual level, what did I experience during this time in my life? What was the overall impression of my spiritual awareness then?

Examples might include a sense of connection and joy, or aloneness, alienation, betrayal, numbness, etc.

_____

_____

_____

_____

_____

_____

Themes and Patterns

What themes do I notice weaving through my experiences from ages seven to twelve?

Refer to the list of themes in the introduction for ideas and examples.

_____

_____

_____

_____

_____

_____

Do I notice any patterns (recurring experiences)?

An example of a pattern might be being picked as a leader at school and at home, being left out of games, and/or experiencing a feeling of not belonging. At this point, we are just noticing themes and patterns to better understand how we were affected by our environment and what we may have decided about ourselves.

_____

_____

_____

_____

_____

_____

On the following page, draw your family. Please don't worry about performing as an artist. Stick figures are perfectly fine. Simply draw how your family relationships felt and what you observed, symbolized by proximity and distance, size of the personalities, and their expressions.

Make a Family Drawing

This drawing represents who felt close to whom, who felt distant, how big someone seemed in contrast to someone else, and the general remembered mood of each of your parents and siblings. Pets, too, can be included, as well as whatever or whoever felt deeply significant to you during your childhood.

What does this drawing tell you about your family dynamics? Who is large,
who is small? Who is close to whom, etc.? What do you feel and think about the
information expressed in your drawing?

_____

_____

_____

_____

_____

_____

On the next page, you are invited to paste photo memories of yourself in your early
years. The child you were still lives inside of you. Honoring your inner child is a
powerful step in reclaiming and, if necessary, healing those parts of yourself.

Photo Memories

My Alchemical Journey: Part One

Now it's time to begin your story. Looking at your life as an alchemist reviewing the ingredients, you will be considering the elements that were "the givens" in your life, your *prima materia*. The *prima materia* will include your birth circumstances, the atmosphere in your home, and your early experience of your parents, grandparents, siblings, peers, and other adult figures that had an impact on you. Which elements were volatile, which were neutral, and which were positive?

In the places in which you don't have recall or enough information, it's okay to create parts of the story from your sense of what occurred, guided by feeling and imagination. Trust yourself. What can factually be proven is not always the point. Your impressions have worth. Your perceptions matter, as you believe them on a deep subconscious level. Fill in the gaps as best you can.

You will be asked to write your journey in three parts: the growing years, your young and mature adult years, and finally your elder years. If you have not reached these later years, you will be writing from a visioning perspective, imagining the best conclusion to the story.

For now, describe the elements your young self encountered in these early years, your *prima materia*.

_____

_____

_____

_____

_____

_____

_____

_____

_____

_____

_____

Part Two

Adolescence—
The Transition

Initiation

The teen years are pivotal in our development. A lot of attention in therapeutic spaces has been given to infant and childhood development, honoring its importance, examining its wounding, and tending to its healing. Very little attention has been focused on adolescence, the crucial transition from childhood to adulthood.

In this momentous period, we first begin to define ourselves and consider our future mission in life. It is a very exciting time of development in which we begin to explore what it means to be an adult, consider more abstract ideas and ideals, and develop our values and our broader philosophy of life. Our bodies change, and we often have our first experiences with serious romantic and erotic attraction. Our standing with peers deeply affects us. What occurs in these seminal experiences colors our perceptions and our hopes and fears regarding relationships, as well as our place in the world moving forward.

Adolescence is a period of heightened emotion and intense sensitivity. We experience a profound desire to fit in with others and find our place. What might seem a small disappointment to an adult can take on enormous significance in the life of a teen. Praise and belonging gives us confidence moving into adulthood, while a demeaning message from peers or adults and a profound heartbreak at this time can leave lasting scars leading to lack of trust in ourselves and others, as well as less than optimal choices as an adult. A network of defenses, perhaps originating in dysfunctional family dynamics earlier on, are reinforced during this period. And, of course, sexual violation and abuse of any sort will devastate trust. Religious taboos also play a part in cultivating shame in what is perfectly natural human development. Natural curiosity, wonder, an innate spirituality, and a sense of the sacred in relationships is often demolished during our teens.

It is also a time of experimentation and risk-taking. In ancient and indigenous cultures, protected yet challenging forms of initiation from childhood into adulthood were and are an established part of the culture. They are largely missing, or at best perfunctory, in our modern western and westernized world. This has made the impulse to test and try out adult behaviors far more dangerous and sometimes even deadly. There are few experienced mentors and elders in place to guide this process.

This new turn on the spiral of time often revisits with a different cast of characters the same themes and wounds of our early childhood. Are we welcomed, accepted, and loved? Are we safe? Who can we trust? Of course, these questions follow us all our lives, but they take on particular weight now. The traumas and dramas of these transitional years don't simply go away in our twenties, thirties, or even in our lifetime. We don't just move on, though we may push those wounds into the mental "basement" for as long as possible. Eventually, however, they sneak out and demand our attention. They may seem to be old history, but if not brought into consciousness, the lingering effects of these adolescent wounds will create the foundation of our subsequent life choices as full-fledged adults. Let's look back to reclaim these crucial years.

When my body was beginning to change, how did I feel about those changes?

If you have a female body, when was your first menstrual period? How was that first experience? How did you feel about the changes in your body and how they compared to other girls?

If you have a male body, when was your first ejaculation, and what did you feel about this change?

_____

_____

_____

_____

_____

_____

If you had a menstrual cycle, how long and how intense were your periods, physically and emotionally? How did you feel about the fact that you bled?

_____

_____

_____

_____

_____

Did I feel supported for who I was and how I was changing? If so, how did I experience that support? In what ways was I not supported during this time? Who supported my changes, and who did not? What effects do I feel this support, or lack of, had on my life?

_____

_____

_____

_____

_____

_____

_____

Was there any sort of celebration of my bodily and emotional changes by my family and/or community?

More recently, especially in the feminist and pagan communities, there has been an effort to bring back a view of the sacredness of menstruation and an honoring of a girl's first bleeding. On a more communal and societal level, Judaism honors adolescence with Bat Mitzvah or Bar Mitzvah ceremonies. In Christianity, confirmation ceremonies serve to mark the same development. In Latin communities, *quinceañeras* celebrate when a girl turns fifteen, honoring her passage into womanhood. More recently, a trend of *quinceañeros* for boys is emerging as a parallel initiation for young men.

Was your coming of age honored? If so, how?

_____

_____

_____

_____

_____

How was my experience of this initiation or celebration?

_____

_____

_____

_____

_____

_____

In many North and South American indigenous tribes, young boys are sent on a solitary, days-long vision quest into the wilderness. The intention is to acquire personal power, possibly encounter a guardian spirit, and find life direction.

The practice of scarification, as well as learning the tribes' legends and spiritual beliefs, are aspects of the Australian aboriginal Bora ceremony. The Samoan Pe'a ceremony of tattooing from torso to knees is another example of initiation into adulthood. Perhaps the tattooing so popular in the twenty-first century unconsciously reflects these more ancient traditions and a resurfacing of something sacred—a powerful statement of stepping visibly into an identity.

For girls, there is often an entrance into a women's clan with its specific duties, responsibilities, and privileges. The Mescalero Apache have a four-day ceremony conferring blessings on the girl as she enters womanhood. A ritualist singer and a female elder preside over the ceremony. For a specified time, the young girl is made into the embodiment of the divine feminine: She who gives birth to all living things. The girl, as the goddess, blesses the community with cattail pollen. Ceremonies like these sacralize the changing status out of childhood, conferring privileges as well as new responsibilities.

For many modern girls, having sex—much of the time prematurely, both emotionally and mentally—is the only significant sign of a change in status besides menstruation. If there were other ways to initiate, value, and honor the emerging woman, perhaps there would be better preparation and less urgency to experience sex prematurely.

If my coming of age wasn't satisfying, uplifting, or empowering, how would I have liked these changes to have been honored? What would have contributed to a greater sense of my dignity, identity, and purpose during that transition?

_____

_____

_____

_____

_____

_____

Relationships at School and at Home in the Teen Years

Because our bodies, minds, and emotions change dramatically between the ages of twelve to eighteen, the responses to the following questions will look different at twelve, fourteen, seventeen, etc. But there might be an overall flavor or essence that comes forward as you consider the answers to the following questions.

During middle school (typically between the ages of eleven to thirteen) how were my relationships with my peers in general? How did I or didn't I fit in? Was I popular or not? Did I have friends or was I mostly a loner? How was that for me?

_____

_____

_____

_____

What was going on in my home at that time? How was that for me?

_____

_____

_____

_____

What do I generally feel about that time in my life?

_____

_____

_____

_____

What did I enjoy most during these years? What gave me a feeling of freedom, agency, and success?

_____

_____

_____

_____

_____

_____

During high school (typically between the ages of fourteen to eighteen), did I find a group I fit in with or not?

_____

_____

_____

_____

_____

Did I have a best friend(s)? If yes, who were they, and why did we get along?

_____

_____

What did we bond over? Did we share common concerns and a similar upbringing? Or were our differences complementary?

_____

_____

_____

_____

_____

What are my fondest memories of them? Do I have any difficult memories?

_____

_____

_____

_____

_____

_____

What was my general reputation in high school? What do I think others thought about me? Did this change or stay consistent throughout those four years?

_____

_____

_____

_____

_____

If my reputation changed, how and why?

_____

_____

_____

_____

Did my peers give me a nickname? How did I feel about that?

_____

_____

_____

_____

Was there a year in which I felt I had definitively emerged from the typically more awkward stage between childhood and teenager? How did that shift impact my life and my conception of self?

_____

_____

_____

_____

_____

_____

What was my relationship with authority figures during this time (teachers, parents, police)? Did it change? If so, why?

_____

_____

_____

_____

_____

_____

_____

What music, books, movies, and other media felt important to me during those years?

_____

_____

_____

_____

_____

How did they influence me? How did they reflect my sense of meaning? How did they impact my beliefs and goals?

_____

_____

_____

_____

_____

_____

_____

Did I have a favorite teacher or another adult who served as an important mentor?

_____

_____

_____

_____

What made that person special and important?

_____

_____

_____

_____

_____

Did I have a favorite subject(s)?

_____

_____

_____

_____

Am I still interested in the same subjects? Have they morphed into related subjects? If not, why?

If not, the answer could be a simple moving on, or disappointment in the material itself. Possibly you were told by a teacher or parent that you weren't good at that subject. This can cut off all interest prematurely.

_____

_____

_____

_____

_____

_____

If you're no longer interested in the subjects you loved as a teen, would you like to rethink leaving any of them behind? What would exploring this subject again look like now?

_____

_____

Did I have a favorite sport or extracurricular activity or hobby as a teenager? What happened to that interest as life progressed?

_____

_____

_____

_____

Would you like to revisit this interest?

_____

_____

Romantic and Sexual Experiences

What were you taught about touching yourself erotically? Did you experience shame and guilt? What did you believe about masturbation as a teen? What do you believe now? Why?

While certain cultures and religions have long condemned self-touch, there have also been others that didn't pathologize exploration and solitary pleasure.

_____

_____

_____

_____

_____

_____

Did I have romantic boyfriends/girlfriends as a teen? Who were they?

_____

_____

_____

_____

_____

_____

Who was the *most* significant romantic relationship and why? What attracted me to that person? What made them special?

_____

_____

_____

_____

_____

_____

What was I looking for in a romantic relationship at the time, either consciously or subconsciously?

_____

_____

_____

_____

If I didn't have a boyfriend/girlfriend as a teenager, was this a personal choice or a decision influenced by outside factors (peers, religious community, parental advice, etc.)?

_____

_____

_____

_____

How did these romantic relationships, or lack thereof, impact my place in my peer group? Did they give me greater or lesser social value? How much did this consideration impact my choices?

_____

_____

_____

_____

_____

If I was in a couple, what common experiences contributed to a shared understanding and trust within our relationship? How were our individual worlds different?

_____

_____

_____

_____

_____

Was I aware of these commonalities and differences at the time or only in retrospect?

_____

_____

What do I make of this information now?

_____

_____

_____

_____

_____

_____

Our first sexual experiences with a partner are often quite complex. Whether it was positive or negative, sex is a profound, "no going back" experience. It creates deep imprints on our identity, as well as a general trust or mistrust of our bodies and in other people as partners.

When and where was my first sexual experience? What was that experience like?

_____

_____

_____

_____

_____

_____

How did that experience affect me moving forward?

_____

_____

_____

_____

_____

_____

Not everyone falls in love in their teens, but if you did, you might consider yourself both lucky and ill-fated. You were an intensely feeling being then and still quite fragile. The ego is just forming during our teenage years, and it's not yet durable enough to navigate the complexity of human emotion.

Falling in love breaks the heart open in a way no other experience can, short of the birth of a child. The ego loses its defenses in the profound beauty and immense possibility of union with another body and soul.

While it is an amazing experience, it's also deeply vulnerable. How that vulnerability is managed has lasting impact, especially in these formative years.

Falling in Love for the First Time

I find myself losing myself in you as if
in some other possible future self,
as if everything has always been waiting
for me in you, in a deep and dazzling,
unexplored nearness, as if someone

waiting at the core of you is anticipating
my arrival in the small hours of your night,
someone who would know me by my first
appearance, if only in shadowed outline,
by my touch, my breath, my whispered words,
about to touch deep inside you, what I was
afraid until now could never be touched in me.[1]

1. David Whyte, "Your Dark Offering," from _David Whyte: Still Possible_, @ 2022 David Whyte. Reprinted with permission from David Whyte and Many Rivers Company, LLC, Langley, WA, www.davidwhyte.com.

Did I fall in love?

_____

_____

_____

_____

_____

_____

How did the relationship go? Were we sexually intimate, and how was that for me? What were my emotions like during this relationship?

_____

_____

_____

_____

_____

_____

_____

_____

What are my happiest memories from this relationship?

_____

_____

_____

_____

_____

What are my most difficult memories from this relationship?

_____

_____

_____

_____

_____

_____

How do I feel that first experience of falling in love affected my sense of confidence, trust, and safety in my body?

_____

_____

_____

_____

_____

_____

_____

As a result of that experience, what did I decide about *myself*? How was my sense of self and my worth impacted?

Rarely, people marry their first love. If, like most, you moved on, did you feel confident and available for the next relationship? Or if your vulnerability and trust were damaged, did you become more self-protective in future relationships as a result? How so?

_____

_____

_____

_____

_____

_____

_____

Did that relationship help me to create healthy boundaries that enhanced future relationships or defensive structures that prevented intimacy?

_____

_____

_____

_____

Have my beliefs about myself and relationships remained the same, or have they shifted and changed over the years? If so, how?

_____

_____

_____

_____

If they have remained the same, would I like them to change? If so, how?

_____

_____

_____

_____

_____

_____

If I experienced betrayal, abandonment, or abuse, what did I do to move forward? Did these coping mechanisms work then? Were they healthy or ultimately poor ways of coping?

_____

_____

_____

_____

Some ways we protect ourselves are by entering a seemingly safe marriage too early, or conversely becoming overly active sexually but without deep intimacy. Maybe we think we are available, but simply can't find the right person. We may have erected an invisible and often unconscious shield. Vulnerability and real intimacy have become too dangerous.

If I am feeling regret, can I forgive myself for choices that were perhaps the only available options to me at the time?

If they were destructive, they were probably the most rapid and effective resources available to you at the time. Just as you were asked to show compassion toward your inner child, do the same for your growing young person.

_____

_____

_____

_____

Do I notice any fallout from these coping strategies, looking back? If so, what do I wish I would have done differently, given the chance? And...what would I do now?

_____

_____

_____

_____

Did my first romantic relationship resemble any of the relationship dynamics I had already experienced with my parents or caregivers?

For example, if you had an elusive, suffocating, or abusive parent, you may have chosen partners with whom you did not risk any real vulnerability. Conversely, you may have had a generally positive experiences of your parents growing up and romantic relationships have been easier territory for you to navigate.

_____

_____

_____

_____

If I had more difficult experiences with either one or both of my parents/caregivers as a child, did I find myself with people who seemed to be the opposite of them at first, only to produce similar feelings of abandonment or betrayal that I experienced growing up?

_____

_____

_____

_____

_____

Did I have any corrective experiences with my first partners?

Corrective experiences heal earlier wounds and negative imprints from the past. An example might be having an absent parent, then being with a partner who consistently shows up for you. This changes your expectations of what is possible in a close relationship and is a healing experience.

_____

_____

_____

_____

What do I know now that I wish I had known then? Is there anything I wish a trusted adult or wise friend would have advised me about at the time?

_____

_____

_____

_____

Can I find any value in these experiences?

For example, did what you experience make you stronger, more self-sufficient, or more selective in your choice of future partners?

_____

_____

_____

_____

_____

_____

_____

_____

_____

The Issue of Addiction

The danger of initiating an addiction is heightened during adolescence. The combination of bodily changes; hypersensitivity to the approval of a peer group, girl or boyfriend; a desire to appear adult; tensions at school, at work, and at home, accompanied by a vulnerable new sense of self, make overindulgence in drink, drugs including smoking, food, or exercise more appealing as a release and solution. We can even be addicted to people. Self-harm through cutting or burning can be immediate but destructive ways to manage helplessness and emotional pain. The effects of these unhealthy coping mechanisms can be lifelong and even lethal.

All addictions represent unmet needs and often the pressure to conform. As Alana Fairchild succinctly points out, "Unraveling an addiction is a journey. It is the same journey we take when we connect with our authentic self and allow it to express freely and without judgment. It is a spiritually demanding task. We need to stop fixating on the addiction and listen for the story beneath it."[1]

Was I addicted to any substance, activity, or person in my teen years? If so, what?

_____

_____

What do I think/feel was the root of this behavior? What lack was I seeking to fill in myself?

Alcohol and drugs are both ways to escape and often begin as a means to fitting in with our peers. Smoking, like alcohol, can be considered adult behavior. Smoking can feel like a satisfying ritual and gives a time out from life. Nicotine has the added benefit of cutting hunger and calming the nerves. It is a method of self-soothing, just as alcohol and marijuana are. Marijuana is commonly used as a means of calming anxiety.

Food addictions often point to a lack of nurturing and good mothering. Overeating fills the lack of emotional nurturance on a physical level and has a numbing effect.

1. Alana Fairchild, *Crystal Stars 11:11*, Blue Angel, 2020, pages 152, 153.

Bulimia can address that same need, but it strives to maintain approval of the thin body by our peers and even at times, our family. To get that deeper need met and still be loved, bulimia allows us "to eat our cake (nurturance) and have it too (not lose the love)."

Anorexia and intense exercise give a sense of control, at least a control of our own bodies in a world in which we feel we have little or no control. Anorexia may also express a wish to disappear entirely. In a culture that overvalues thinness and physical appearance and prowess in general, these addictions can provide desired social acceptance. Intense exercise has an added benefit of increasing feel good endorphins that serve to tune out emotional and mental pain.

Cutting and any form of obvious self-harm is a way to distract from emotional pain by replacing it with physical sensation and preoccupation.

Consider now what could have been the bigger story behind "too much" or "too little"? What were you trying to soothe and fix by resorting to these addictions? Were you filling a sense of emptiness and if so, describe what that could have been about. Rather than pathologizing yourself, look for the deeper story and need.

What pain was I looking to relieve through satisfying my addiction? What does my addiction tell me about my soul's deep need at that time?

_____
_____
_____
_____
_____
_____

If I could have benefited from some kind of support through this passage. what would that have looked like?

_____
_____
_____
_____
_____
_____

Values, Spirituality, and Philosophy of Life

What values were especially important to me as a teenager?

Generally, we can identify our values by what we feel is important to us. But we can also identify them by the instinctive anger we experience when a specific value is not being honored. For example, if justice was important to you, maybe you realized this when you witnessed an injustice. If freedom is important to you, you realized this value when you witnessed others being oppressed. If safety is a strong value, you may notice a focus on security. Maybe loyalty was and is nonnegotiable. What were and maybe still are your core values?

_____

_____

_____

_____

_____

_____

Are these values still important to me?

_____

_____

_____

_____

Did I share the same basic values as most of my peer group or did some or all of them differ? How were they different, and what made me notice these differences?

_____

_____

_____

_____

Were my values basically the same or markedly different from the adults in my family, my community, and/or others in authority (at school and in society at large)?

It could be that your family supported certain shared values that differed from the surrounding community. Or, conversely, the situation might have been more homogenous (i.e., every sphere of your life sharing the same values) or more complex (shared values with your peers but not your bigger community or your family).

_____

_____

_____

_____

_____

_____

What values did I share with my family of origin at this point in my life? Which ones differed?

_____

_____

_____

_____

_____

If my values were different, what was that like for me? How did I cope with these differences?

_____

_____

_____

_____

_____

_____

Are my friendships today reflections of values that have remained important to me since I was a teenager? How have my values changed or stayed the same?

_____

_____

_____

_____

_____

Spirituality and Philosophy

Spirituality can be expressed within a religious frame, but it is not limited to religion. Spirituality is found in what we value most, what we experience as sacred, and what gives our lives meaning in a more global and sometimes transcendental way.

Some examples of spirituality outside of a formalized religion include nature as a source of spiritual connection, the feeling of service to humanity, philosophical and scientific revelations, or a profound connection with a beloved.

Did I have an interest in religion, spirituality, or philosophy in my teens? If so, how would I describe my spirituality and life philosophy during my adolescence?

_____

_____

_____

_____

_____

Do I recall any experiences of awe and wonder? What were these moments like?

_____

_____

_____

_____

_____

_____

Is there an age that I remember becoming "conscious," waking up to myself as an individual person aware of the complexity of my surroundings?

Maybe this awakening was gradual, or maybe it was instantaneous. This moment might have occurred in childhood or adolescence.

_____

_____

_____

_____

Can you trace a connective thread between your spirituality and philosophy growing up and how it manifests now? Perhaps you considered yourself religious, but you now consider yourself spiritual. Maybe you see a thread of mystical temperament that has remained with you despite all that has changed in your life. Or perhaps you've always aimed to make the world a better place. Maybe you've always prioritized philosophical study or a humanist philosophy. Can you spot the emerging themes?

_____

_____

_____

_____

_____

_____

Four Spiritual Paths

The more than 5,000-year-old spiritual philosophy of Hinduism describes four paths of evolution that we can apply to ourselves and our temperament, whatever our belief system. It makes clear that each of the paths, though different, lead to the same destination and goal. One can be a practitioner of all or several, but usually there is one or two that most suits our temperament.

Bhakti yoga is an emotion-based path of the heart, of devotion. *Jñāna yoga* is a scholars' path, finding a route to spirit through the intellect. *Karma yoga* is a path of action that focuses on acts of service and good works. Finally, *Raja Yoga*, the path of the intuition, is the path of the mystics and usually includes at least some of the other paths.

If I were to assign myself a primary and secondary path, which two feel the most resonant?

_____

_____

_____

_____

How did these natural tendencies manifest as a teen?

_____

_____

_____

_____

_____

Memories, Themes, and Patterns

What are my best memories from this time?

_____

_____

_____

_____

_____

_____

How did these memories influence my life moving forward?

_____

_____

_____

_____

_____

_____

What are my most difficult memories from my teenage years?

_____

_____

_____

_____

_____

_____

How did these memories influence my life moving forward?

_____

_____

_____

_____

_____

_____

Have I been able to come to peace with these experiences?

Coming to peace with these events may take years, but the question is offered here for consideration.

_____

_____

_____

_____

_____

_____

_____

_____

_____

_____

Remember to take good care of yourself as you do this work. If you are experiencing grief or anger, consider processing your feelings further through writing in your journal. Don't forget to use the tools from your self-care, reset list.

What recurring themes do I notice in reviewing my teen years?

_____

_____

_____

_____

_____

_____

It might be too soon to identify, but am I beginning to notice any recurring patterns? If so, what are these patterns?

_____

_____

_____

_____

_____

_____

Checking In

The Body

What general feeling, tone, or experience did I have of my body as a teenager? Some examples include experiencing your body as strong/vibrant, sensual, beautiful, awkward/ugly, weak/insufficient, awkward, damaged, or as an obstacle. There will probably be a combination of experiences.

_____

_____

_____

_____

Was I able to love and appreciate my body as a teen?

Because we are very sensitive to acceptance and rejection by others at this age, even someone who might socially be considered attractive can suffer from terrible self-judgment and body dysmorphia, leading to eating disorders and other addictions. This situation is far worse for many who do not meet the standards of attractiveness in a particular culture.

_____

_____

_____

_____

What were ways that I compensated for any feelings of not being good enough?

Besides addictions, people often use overachievement in any area to prove worth and lovability. Maybe you had to be the top of your class, the funniest or coolest person, or most athletically exceptional?

_____

_____

_____

_____

_____

_____

Do you recognize your intrinsic worth now, regardless of achievements? Where are you in that process?

_____

_____

_____

_____

The Heart

What was my experience on a heart level? Some examples might include open, joyful, fearful, sensitive, confused, broken, sad, or helpless. Use these or your own descriptions. We are complex creatures. Your answer may include many descriptions.

_____

_____

_____

_____

_____

The Mind

What was the general tenor of my thoughts? Examples might include excited, stimulated, creative, inspired, confused, anxious, depressed, hypervigilant, etc.

_____

_____

_____

_____

_____

_____

The Spirit

What did I experience on a spiritual level as a teen? Examples might include a sense of connection and joy or, alternatively, alienation, disconnection, numbness, etc.

_____

_____

_____

_____

_____

_____

The Wise Mind

Dialectical Behavioral Therapy uses the idea of "the wise mind" to discover a broader and more elevated view of a situation. If your experience as a teenager negatively affected your self-esteem and basic trust in others and yourself, ask your wise mind for counsel.

The wise mind can be imagined as your guide, your higher self, or your soul. Any of these names can work. Which feels right for you?

What does my _____ want to tell me about my experiences as a teen? Use any of these names for the part of us that knows more than our conscious ego.

Can it show me the value in what happened? What does it want to tell me about myself during those years?

Remember that wisdom is always compassionate and does not blame or scold. If you hear the voice of recrimination, it is *not* the voice of the wise mind, guide, higher self, or your soul.

_____

_____

_____

_____

_____

_____

_____

Go through this same exercise of asking for wisdom if you were violated or abused at *any* age. Consider the wise mind by whatever name, as your best, most compassionate, and most intelligent friend.

Write that message here.

My wise mind wants to tell me this about the experience(s):

_____

_____

_____

_____

_____

_____

_____

This is what my wise mind wants to tell me about my true worth:

_____

_____

_____

_____

_____

_____

If the wise mind or guide told you positive things about yourself, consider whether you ever speak to yourself that kindly. If you don't usually feel this compassionate toward yourself, then you have proof that you did not simply make-up this message. It is coming from a deeper part or wiser source than your conscious mind.

What we have explored so far may very well have included experiences of trauma, both in childhood and adolescence. Trauma is experienced when we feel deeply unsafe and helpless. Traumatic patterning often gets stuck in the brain rather than being processed. It also becomes lodged in our muscles, tissues, and organs. We are complex creatures with information traveling seamlessly between mind and body.

In this workbook, we are addressing memory. Memory is not only stored in the mind. It lives in our bodies as well. Somatic therapy can powerfully release the lingering effects of trauma on our nervous system, endocrine system, and muscular system. Releasing trauma from the body itself is a highly beneficial addition to this workbook. We will cover more information on trauma later, and you'll find resources for further help in the Resource section at the end.

An Introduction to Shadow Work

Again and again, our goddesses and heroines travel to the underworld. Again and again, we descend in our own lives. Why do we tell this story over and over again? The underworld is where we confront the wounded, exiled pieces of ourselves. The pieces we'd forgotten, hidden, or didn't want to see in the first place.

—Amanda Yates Garcia, *Initiation*

Our shadow contains traits we have rejected, either because of culture, parents, or religion, as well as experiences that caused us pain or loss of love. Often, we decide to reject the negative expressions of neutral qualities we saw in our parents and siblings. We relegate those qualities to the metaphoric back closet or underworld in our psyche. Along with the givens of our birth, they are our *prima materia*. They live under the radar, in the dark of the subconscious, and have a subliminal but powerful impact on our lives.

Let's say you had a parent who was so self-involved that they could not see or value you. Perhaps that parent demanded constant attention and control. Maybe you witnessed the damage that this narcissism incurred—for you, for your relationship with them, for their outside friendships, and in their work environments. You decided to be anything but a narcissist, and perhaps stepped away from even healthy self-love, self-care, and confidence as a result. You became too self-effacing and sacrificial to avoid any hint of narcissism.

Or perhaps you had a volatile parent and may have witnessed their abuse of power, so you decided that power itself, and especially anger, was highly dangerous. Maybe you also decided any form of leadership might lead to abuse of power, and safety was only insured by staying mostly invisible.

If you encountered persistent criticism from your parents or siblings, your self-confidence and self-esteem were assaulted. Maybe this led to a lack of self-trust and healthy discernment. The list of examples could go on and on.

The qualities we experienced negatively, however, do not go away with our attempts to distance ourselves from them. They become repressed in us, but find expression in the people we meet, retriggering the pain. The classical interpretation is that whenever we constellate psychic energy, we will find that energy repeated again and again in our experience. Depth psychology explains this recurring cycle as our psyche looking for *wholeness*. We will encounter similar situations until we resolve the complex.

When we notice qualities we despise in others, usually resulting from pain in our past, an internal warning light goes on. We want nothing to do with that situation again. But the truth is that we can only move forward in our development if we come to terms with these qualities, finding their healthy expression inside of us. Until this occurs, we are perpetually haunted by that which we label as unacceptable. We find ourselves, unwittingly, with a boss, a coworker (or several), a partner, or a roommate who expresses the same distortion we saw in our parents early on. Until we face this pattern head on, we rarely escape that same quality emerging in one situation or another.

The Shadow We Inherit

Just as your physical body is an utterly new expression—composed of two lines of ancestral heritage spanning thousands, even millions of years—so too your psyche includes ancestral expressions seeking a unique identity. This marriage of qualities often feels quite rough at the start.

Imagine an orchestra made up of many diverse instruments and musicians. This orchestra can create a cacophony or the most beautiful music. It has the potential for both. There is a part of you that is the conductor, your consciousness. Do you choose to silence parts of the orchestra, or do you decide to integrate their parts into the glorious symphony of your life? Every attribute we repress is still part of the orchestra. Even dissonant notes can add interest and value to the music. Finding how best to conduct this part of your orchestra is an invitation into consciousness and a bigger, more whole self. Every conductor has their work cut out for them in finding each part's healthy expression, but once the work is done, this music can be passed on to those around you, to your children if you have them, and to humanity as a whole.

None of us is entirely isolated, even if we choose the hermit's life. We are not separate beings, flung into a short incarnation. We are an integral part of the greater humanity. What we emanate, the music we play, sends ripples through the whole. Thus, shadow work is a powerful contribution not only to our personal development but to the expression of a greater humanity as well.

To assist you in this shadow work, consider the following questions. You may not have consciously made the decision to distance yourself from certain attributes, but in retrospect, you can identify unconscious choices you've made in reaction to the pain of these distorted expressions.

What qualities in your parents did you feel caused suffering when you were growing up? What did you wish hadn't been true about them? If you were adopted or had stepparents or foster parents, they, too, played "instruments" that are now a part of your orchestra. Even though they don't represent your biological inheritance, they created part or all of your home environment growing up. From a spiritual perspective, they are chosen to add their parts to your life's symphony—to contribute yet another layer of symphonic potential. Nurture and nature both play a part.

When I was growing up, I noticed my mother was _____, and I decided never to be _____.

When I was growing up, I noticed my father was_____, and I decided never to be _____.

If you had stepparents or foster parents/guardians:

I noticed this mother figure was_____, and I decided never to be _____.

I noticed this father figure was _____, and I decided never to be_____.

Now consider what might be positive expressions of each of the above attributes.

For example, narcissism can be modified into *positive self-love and self-worth*, knowing that you are as deserving as anyone else. Negative expressions of power, in a positive light, might be expressed as *leadership and standing up against injustice*. Greed could be positively worked into *healthy enjoyment* of the gift of life. Laziness or slowness could be modified into *mindfulness, patience*, and the ability to slow down to appreciate and connect with life more deeply. Passivity in a parent might be tempered into *gentleness and peace*.

Notice if you have pushed away the positive expressions of your parents' and siblings' characteristics in your attempts to dismantle the effects of their negative expressions. Notice what the lack of those positive transformations have done to the quality of your life. Now consider how including them in a *healthy expression* could add value and greater complexity and beauty to your world.

In seeking wholeness, we are invited to include not only what we consider positive qualities but also those qualities we dislike or fear. Shadow work invites us to be *all* of who we can be in this wonderous opportunity of a life.

Our Family Shadows

Psychiatrist Murray Bowen invented the genogram in his family systems theory in the 1970s. This tool is extremely valuable in understanding our inherited ancestral patterns. The genogram is not only a classic family tree documenting marriages, births, divorces, and deaths, it also includes details like ancestors' reputations, the dynamics between siblings and with one's parents, severe illness and handicaps, abortions and miscarriages, addictions, and suicides, etc. This exercise is extremely informative in revealing "shadow" patterns that get repeated through the generations. Genogram templates are easily accessed online, and working through it can be highly informative and useful as an adjunct to this workbook.

Sara Wiseman continues this work with her program, The Family Karma Project (sarawiseman.com). She identifies seven shadows in the family: abuse, addiction, violence, poverty, illness, abandonment, and betrayal. Her work offers useful exploratory questions and suggestions for healing.

Photo Memories

On the following page, paste photographs or make drawings that evoke your teen years. Alternatively, you could put some photos up where you can see them (maybe on your dedicated altar) to honor who you were then. You can honor that time in your life whether it is remembered as a mostly positive or mostly negative time, or a mixture of both. Your teen self was tender, vulnerable, possibly philosophical, sensitive, and very likely quite creative. In the project of learning to love and honor the self, it is wonderfully helpful to remember and reclaim the many versions of ourselves that have traversed the years.

Just as we all have an inner child, we also have an inner adolescent who needs our acceptance and our love. Including them in our understanding of who we've become enriches us, no matter what stage of life we're in.

Let's move forward into part two of your journey. Continue from where you left off in the narrative of your childhood. What happened next?

My Alchemical Journey, Part Two

Making "Gold out of Lead" or "Flowers out of Compost"

What were your pivotal experiences, positive and negative, as you grew out of childhood into young adulthood? If you had difficult experiences, how did they affect you? Maybe you are still managing some of the fallout from that time. But our wounds often lead to our positive contributions to life. As humans, we are meaning makers of our experience. Are you able to observe these experiences from a more objective perspective, extracting a valuable essence to carry into the future?

The goal is to work with the *prima materia* of these experiences, not to suppress or repress them. Instead, with an alchemist's care, we are invited to refine them into elements that serve us as well as our relationships. If the pain is present, are you able to witness it? Can you let it flow through you, without clinging and becoming stuck in identification with it? Have you been able to partially or even fully transmute this *prima materia*?

Perhaps you are already expressing that potential in your career or with friends and family. Perhaps you have already managed to gather wisdom from whatever journeys you have taken into the more difficult aspects of human experience.

These were my most difficult experiences. How have they affected my life? In what ways?

How have I been able to alchemize these experiences? Is there still more work to do?

_____

_____

_____

_____

_____

_____

_____

Part Three

Adulthood

Young Adulthood: Experimenting, the 20s

Work

In my twenties, did I know who I wanted to be and what I wanted to do with my life? If so, was I able to consciously choose and pursue that goal from the beginning? Or, alternatively, was I exploring in my twenties?

It is more usual to *not* know the answers to these questions until later in life, and it is common to change direction after having had some experience too.

_____

_____

_____

_____

_____

_____

Did I feel prepared to enter the work world? If not, what preparation do I wish I would have had?

_____

_____

_____

_____

These were my first jobs (including any jobs I had as a teen):

_____

_____

_____

_____

_____

_____

_____

What jobs did I enjoy, and what jobs did I dislike the most? Why?

These early experiences help us recognize what we are and are not suited to do, as well as what we enjoy and what we don't want to spend our time doing.

_____

_____

_____

_____

_____

_____

_____

_____

What did I learn about myself in these work environments? What was easy, and what wasn't?

Consider what you learned that helped you move forward into adulthood.

_____

_____

_____

_____

_____

_____

If I wasn't traditionally employed, what did I spend my time doing in my twenties? This might include continuing schooling, beginning a family, doing an internship, pursuing entrepreneurship, traveling, caregiving for a family member, etc.

_____

_____

_____

_____

_____

If you were in school during your twenties:

How do I feel about this time now? Was I studying what I wanted to study?

_____

_____

_____

_____

_____

_____

From my current perspective, how do I think these experiences helped me grow?

Both pleasant and unpleasant experiences help us to discover more of who we are and what we want in life.

_____

_____

_____

_____

_____

_____

_____

Consider the relationships you had with your employers or instructors during your twenties.

How did my employers/instructors treat me? What was the feedback I received about my value?

_____

_____

_____

_____

_____

_____

_____

Who supported my development and in what ways? Who were my best teachers/ mentors in the work world?

_____

_____

_____

_____

_____

_____

_____

What did I question or decide about my capabilities and my value based on these experiences?

_____

_____

_____

_____

_____

_____

How were my relationships with my coworkers or fellow students?

_____

_____

_____

_____

_____

Were there any similar relationship dynamics from my family repeated in these early work or school relationships with bosses and coworkers, and/or my professors and fellow students? Or, conversely, did these patterns change and was there welcome healing in those previous dynamics?

Work environments (and school environments) often replicate family structures, including sibling rivalries and parental/child relationships. Consider whether your experiences in any way repeated the dynamics you experienced in your family growing up—only this time with bosses and coworkers or professors and fellow students.

_____

_____

_____

_____

_____

_____

_____

_____

A Calling

A calling, or vocation, is a deep impulse toward a particular interest. Some callings are well defined, like the calling to become a doctor or nurse, a monk, an advocate for social justice, an artist, a parent, etc. Some callings, however, are more esoteric, less defined by our culture, and harder to pin down. Perhaps you are fascinated by astronomy, literature, philosophy, religion, metaphysics, ancient history, or archaeology, but you don't necessarily want to (or may not be able to) pursue an academic and/or professional career in these areas. Sometimes you can and do follow these interests even when the world tells you they are impractical.

Callings are mysterious and often carry a sense of what Carl Jung called the "numinous" (a sense of mystery and meaning) about them. We experience them as intensely personal, even spiritual, and awesome in quality. The ancient Greeks imagined these callings coming from a spiritual source they called the "Daimon." Socrates often spoke with his Daimon, and so did Jung, in the person he visualized as a wise seer whom he called "Philemon."

The Daimon has been equated with the higher self, the soul, and the holy guardian angel. But these higher powers are not the pure "sweetness and light" figures that are typical of Christianity's view of angels. The Daimon is a powerful, towering imperative that demands we be true to our soul and its mission.

Not everyone feels a call from, or a personal connection with, a Daimon, but this concept is a useful way to envision the insistence we sometimes feel toward pursuing a certain study or goal, often despite the lack of understanding from family, the prevailing culture, or even our conscious mind. Maybe you began to feel the stirrings of an interest in childhood, and you still hear it or perhaps have had to put it on hold as you entered the real world.

What are my thoughts about a personal calling and/or a Daimon?

_____

_____

_____

_____

_____

_____

_____

_____

If I can relate to the idea of a calling and/or a Daimon, what was my relationship to it in my twenties? Did I feel like I had outside support for this calling?

_____

_____

_____

_____

_____

_____

If I felt sidetracked from what felt like my true path in my twenties (whether I knew what that was yet or not), can I find learning and meaning in the detour?

_____

_____

_____

_____

_____

_____

Have I been able to find a way to answer the calling in some way, even if I took another job or professional route? If not, how do I feel about that?

_____

_____

_____

_____

_____

_____

Relationships—Friends and Lovers

What are/were/have been my most memorable relationships during this decade?

Include both romantic and platonic relationships.

_____
_____
_____
_____
_____
_____
_____
_____
_____

What happened with these relationships?

_____
_____
_____
_____
_____
_____
_____

Did I fall in love?

_____
_____
_____
_____

What attracted me to this person(s)?

_____

_____

_____

_____

_____

Why were each of these relationships important? How did they reflect who I was at the time? How did they serve my growth or sense of security? Do I still know any of these people?

_____

_____

_____

_____

_____

_____

_____

_____

Did I remain single or was I with a partner(s)? If I had a committed partnership, what drew me to joining my life with that specific person?

_____

_____

_____

_____

_____

_____

_____

I chose to partner (or not) because:

_____

_____

_____

_____

_____

_____

_____

If I had a committed relationship, was I trying to emulate the positive model of my parents' marriage, or were my choices seeking the opposite experience, possibly in reaction to their marriage? How did that work out?

_____

_____

_____

_____

_____

_____

What did I learn about myself from those experience(s)?

_____

_____

_____

_____

_____

_____

The following questions only apply if you had a child:

As a young parent, did I feel I had support, emotionally and practically? If so, from whom? If not, how did I feel about that? How did I manage?

_____

_____

_____

_____

_____

_____

How did I feel about being a parent? Did I feel it was the right choice for me or not? Why?

_____

_____

_____

_____

_____

_____

Did I feel any fears, regrets, or doubts about my decision to be a parent?

This is a big question. You may need to continue writing about this in a journal.

_____

_____

_____

_____

_____

_____

Did I experience a miscarriage or abortion? Did I decide to give up a child for adoption at this time in my life? What was my experience of this like? Did I feel supported?

Again, this and the following questions may provoke intense feeling. You may need more room to process. Please take care of yourself in this work.

> If you need to skip over this section until you have support, then do so. Your well-being and groundedness are the most important pieces of this work. Remember your self-care, reset list, and use it when needed.

If I felt guilt or grief, did I give myself space to process and mourn?

If not then, it's not too late now. Often, though the mind is clear, the body and the heart grieve. If you feel guilt, you might write a letter to the soul of the unborn child and put it on your altar or alternatively release it to the sky in a balloon. I believe a sincere prayer of the heart never goes unheard.

_____

_____

_____

What are my beliefs about miscarriage? What are my beliefs about abortion?

_____

_____

_____

_____

_____

_____

Where did these beliefs originate? Are they the same now? If my beliefs have changed, how so? Why?

_____

_____

_____

_____

_____

_____

_____

How did these events change me?

_____

_____

_____

_____

_____

_____

_____

_____

What was the general tone of my life during these years?

_____

_____

_____

_____

_____

What sustained me in my twenties?

This could be any special relationships you had with a person, place, an animal, and/or a spiritual tradition.

_____

_____

_____

_____

_____

_____

_____

_____

Imagine different roads not taken at this time of life. What choices might I have made instead?

_____

_____

_____

_____

_____

_____

_____

_____

_____

Can I find value in the choices I did make, leading me to the next chapter in my life?

_____

_____

_____

_____

_____

Looking back and observing the challenges I faced at the start of my adult life, can I feel compassion for myself? From the point of view of my more mature self, can I appreciate my learning and growth during this time?

If pain resulted from your choices, recognize that you were young and likely had little or no psychological training. Possibly you didn't have the resources to make any other choice. In any case, we usually carry a very incomplete map of adult terrain in our twenties.

_____

_____

_____

_____

_____

Middle Adulthood (30s-50s)—Allegiances and Alliances

The Journey

One day you finally knew
what you had to do, and began,
though the voices around you
kept shouting
their bad advice—
though the whole house
began to tremble
and you felt the old tug
at your ankles.
"Mend my life!"
each voice cried.
But you didn't stop.
You knew what you had to do,
though the wind pried
with its stiff fingers
at the very foundations,
though their melancholy
was terrible.
It was already late
enough, and a wild night,
and the road full of fallen
branches and stones.
But little by little,
as you left their voices behind
the stars began to burn
through the sheets of clouds,
and there was a new voice
which you slowly
recognized as your own,
that kept you company
as you strode deeper and deeper
into the world,

determined to do
the only thing you could do–
determined to save
the only life you could save.[1]

Work and Service

This section includes jobs, professions, being a stay-at-home parent, and/or being a primary caregiver to a family member. These questions explore our service to others and our participation in community, as well as our ability to support ourselves.

Where have I worked? What were my job title(s)? What is a general description of my responsibilities during this time?

If you went back to school for further training, list this as well.

_____

_____

_____

_____

Did/do these jobs feel like a contribution to my life, another person's life, an animal's life, my society, or the natural world?

Examples include all forms of the service and retail industry, caregiving, hospitality, medical jobs, and professions including veterinarians, architects, real estate agents, gardeners and farmers, mechanics, the garment industry, etc. With the positive intention of service, almost any job can offer value.

_____

_____

_____

_____

1. Mary Oliver, "The Journey," *New and Selected Poems, Vol. 1*, Beacon Press, 1992.

Have these jobs provided me with an arena for self-expression?

_____

_____

_____

_____

_____

_____

During the past decade, did I learn more about my gifts, as well what does not resonate well with me? What does and doesn't suit me? In what capacities do I flourish and help others to flourish?

_____

_____

_____

_____

_____

_____

_____

_____

If I felt like I had a vocation, a calling, to a particular form of work or service, have I been able to follow that calling? Did/do I feel supported by family, friends, and community to do so?

_____

_____

_____

_____

If I haven't been able to satisfy this calling or pursue talents that bring me joy
and satisfaction while in the workplace, what ways have I found to express them
outside the formal work environment?

_____

_____

_____

_____

_____

_____

Relationships in the Workplace

What has/have been my experience(s) with authorities and mentors in the
workplace in my thirties? Were my employers helpful/supportive, antagonistic/
punitive, domineering/abusive?

Can I identify any relationship dynamics and/or patterns I experienced in my
childhood that repeated themselves in the workplace as an adult?

_____

_____

_____

_____

_____

_____

_____

Did I notice any changes in myself as I grew older and more experienced?

Maybe you simply matured. Maybe you had a corrective experience, in which you expected the worst from someone and were pleasantly surprised by a healthier, more positive outcome.

_____
_____
_____
_____
_____
_____

How about my experience with coworkers? What, if any, similarities did I notice between how I related to them and how I related to my siblings or classmates growing up?

_____
_____
_____
_____
_____
_____

What are my takeaways from these experiences? Did my workplace interactions change how I view safety, trust, support, cooperation, teamwork, and competition in the workplace?

_____
_____
_____

What value do I bring to the workplace (to my colleagues, my industry, and my profession)?

_____

_____

_____

_____

How do I see myself in relationship to the workplace community: valued and valuable, or inconsequential and overlooked?

_____

_____

_____

_____

Do I like to work on my own, to oversee my own schedule and be my own boss, or do I prefer working with a team? Do I prefer a structured or unstructured environment? What does this information tell me about myself?

_____

_____

_____

_____

_____

Do I have any regrets regarding my work? What are they?

Though this question seems negative, it aims to reveal how much you've come to know yourself through your experiences.

_____

_____

_____

_____

_____

_____

If I had the chance to do things differently in my career/workplace, what new choices would I make?

_____

_____

_____

_____

What do I imagine might have been the gifts of making those different choices?

_____

_____

_____

_____

What do I imagine I would have felt if I'd made those choices?

_____

_____

_____

_____

If I would've made other choices regarding my career/workplace, what stopped me from making them (e.g., fear, lack of information, lack of support, etc.)?

_____

_____

_____

_____

Are those imagined choices realistic in retrospect, considering my life circumstances and what I knew at the time?

_____
_____
_____
_____

If, realistically, I couldn't have gone in another direction, do I understand and accept the choices I did make (or were made for me)?

_____
_____
_____
_____
_____
_____

Is there any way that I can live into those lost possibilities or some modified version of them now?

_____
_____
_____
_____
_____
_____

What gifts have resulted from the choices I *did* make (or were made for me)?

These gifts can be either direct or indirect (for example, increased patience or discipline, or an increased appreciation of kindness, an acceptance of differences, etc.). Often, we learn who we want to be and what we want to do by discovering who we *don't* want to be and what we *don't* want to do.

_____

_____

_____

_____

_____

_____

_____

_____

My Relationship to Money

Money is a neutral resource, a simplified form of exchange, but our attitude toward money greatly impacts whether it comes easily to us or not. We may think we want to make money but have the subconscious beliefs that "money is the root of all evil," "the rich rob the poor," "money is the result of a corrupt system," "filthy lucre," "I don't deserve it," etc. Or maybe you think of money as offering you freedom, security, and a sense of personal value.

What do I believe about money and why?

_____

_____

_____

_____

_____

_____

How did my upbringing influence these thoughts and beliefs?

_____

_____

_____

_____

Is my relationship with money in balance?

_____

_____

_____

_____

_____

_____

Do my beliefs about money enhance or detract from my life experiences? Have I questioned these beliefs?

_____

_____

_____

_____

_____

_____

Would you like to rewrite any of these beliefs? You are invited to do so here.

_____

_____

_____

_____

_____

_____

If you are preoccupied with money, write about why you think that is, from a psychological perspective. An example might be that you don't have enough money and want the freedom it offers. Maybe you are focused on it because you have not felt safe or been adequately valued by others. Maybe you are hoping that money will earn you respect and social value.

Conversely, you may be averse to touching money because you believe money will make you a bad person and your self-esteem feels shaky. Perhaps you struggle with the ability to receive. Maybe you see yourself as the struggling artist always seeking a patron. Maybe you resent the lack of respect and inequality that a culture based on money has produced. Maybe you believe if you are unconventional and an outsider, you must pay the price.

Or you may struggle between two opposing forces: over-giving and then withholding or overcharging. This conflict can generate resentment, which creates an invisible wall preventing abundance.

What beliefs have you inhereited from your parents and the surrounding culture?

These are just examples. Write your own ideas below. There may be more than one reason for your thoughts on receiving and spending money, and they may be conflicting. The aim here is honesty, regardless of how you currently handle money (or don't).

_____
_____
_____
_____
_____
_____
_____
_____
_____
_____
_____

Do you overspend? Why?

_____
_____
_____
_____

What do I want my relationship with money and finances to be?

If a shift is needed, imagine it now. Who would you like to be in relationship to money and why? See yourself in a positive rather than a conflicting relationship. Write about that experience below.

_____

_____

_____

_____

_____

_____

Are there any steps I can take to make that vision a reality?

_____

_____

_____

_____

_____

Has managing money helped you to grow responsibility?

_____

_____

Relationships: Friends and Lovers

Friendships

What are/were my most significant friendships during this period of my life (thirties through fifties)?

_____

_____

_____

_____

_____

_____

_____

_____

What brings/brought us together?

Your answer might include shared interests, values, and/or simple chemistry and affinity. Can you explain this chemistry/affinity, or is it somehow inexplicable but nevertheless present?

What qualities do you especially associate with each of these friendships (examples might include exciting discussions, shared values and goals, playfulness, humor, loyalty and dedication, trust, inspiration, creativity, shared background, shared love of nature, shared love of a certain subject, shared trauma, etc.)?

_____

_____

_____

_____

_____

_____

_____

_____

What is the nourishing quality I most experience with each person? What part of me emerges most strongly in each relationship?

_____
_____
_____
_____
_____
_____
_____
_____

If a friendship ended, did it dissolve naturally or was it difficult?

_____
_____
_____
_____
_____
_____

If there have been any significant experiences of loss and grief in these relationships, what happened?

_____
_____
_____
_____
_____
_____
_____

What did I make of what occurred? How did I come to terms with the ending? Did I feel any feelings I remember experiencing earlier in life?

_____

_____

_____

_____

_____

_____

_____

_____

_____

Again, putting myself in the role of screenwriter, can I envision other possible endings to these stories? If these friendships needed to end, what might have been a more satisfying conclusion to these relationships?

_____

_____

_____

_____

_____

_____

_____

_____

_____

Would these endings have been possible? Or, having done this exercise, am I able to see an inevitability to the way things ended? Does this perspective bring me greater peace and acceptance of this loss?

_____

_____

_____

_____

_____

_____

_____

Have these experiences negatively affected my feelings of safety and trust in others and myself? If so, would I like to heal? What would this healing look like?

Imagine what a healed you would look and feel like. How would that you move forward with life?

_____

_____

_____

_____

_____

Is it possible to heal the relationship? If not, what can I do to promote my own healing and progress moving forward?

_____

_____

_____

_____

_____

_____

_____

What have I learned as a result of these experiences? What have I done with this *prima materia*?

Consider whether a betrayal might've helped you become more discerning. Maybe you more highly value your other loyal friendships? Perhaps the disappointed expectations you experienced resulted in greater acceptance. Heartbreaks can open us to greater empathy and self-care.

_____

_____

_____

_____

_____

_____

A Shift in Frequency

Often, when a significant relationship ends, another comes in that is an upgrade in terms of a shared connection, especially if we are changing directions, or have personally grown and healed past wounds. Friendships require at least some aspects of a shared life and worldview. If there are no longer enough commonalities, we tend to find ourselves drifting apart.

This exercise is not meant to objectify the people in our lives but rather to notice how, who, and what we need tends to show up as we grow and change. Sometimes, we change our "frequency," much like changing radio stations, and the people in our lives are still on the earlier "channel." This doesn't make them bad or wrong, they're just no longer the right match.

A person with whom you used to share a great deal of laughter might upgrade to a new person who provides you with the same sense of fun but is more resonant, supportive, and safer now than your old friend. Consider the shifts in your relationships over these middle decades. Can you spot how your relationships have shifted with your "change in frequency" (a shift in interests or your growth)?

We may be heading in different directions, but we are each on the right road for our learning. If you have had to let someone go, it's best to thank and bless them, at least in your heart, as you part ways.

What have I learned is important to me now in the realms of friendship? What qualities am I looking for in the people who will be coming into my life?

_____

_____

_____

_____

_____

_____

_____

Intimate Relationships—Seeking the Ideal Other

The Anima and Animus

Jung noted that we tend to seek out our contrasting complement, "the special other," for a partner. In Jungian terms, the complement of the masculine psyche is the *anima*, while the *animus* complements the feminine. For a boy, his mother is the first experience of the *anima*, while a girl experiences her father as her first *animus*. The *anima* or *animus* image that lives inside us, the complementary other, is largely unconscious and idealized. It is important to note that both the *anima* and *animus* can have any of the traditional definitions of feminine and masculine traits.

It is possible and even common to have more than one *animus* or *anima* living in our psyche. Jung himself is an example of this with his marriage to Emma and his long-standing relationship with Toni Wolff, two very different women. While Emma aligned more closely with his traditional Swiss values and culture embodied by his mother, Toni was a new incarnation of his more exotic nurse (nanny), and with whom he felt great warmth, love, and safety as a young child.

Considering potential partners, we may discover that we are attracted to someone who personifies the overt qualities in a parent or guardian, or to someone who expresses their *unlived* side. A woman whose father was a captain of industry, a CEO, or a political figure, may look for a powerful leader. Alternatively, a woman with that same father might be drawn to the opposite type—someone who expresses the repressed poetic or musical nature in her father—and go for an Orpheus (poet/musician).

We can see an example of both dynamics at play in Prince Harry's marriage to Meghan Markle. Meghan lives out both Diana's unwillingness to conform and her ease with the public, as well as Diana's unrealized dream to be more fully self-expressed and free of the terrific weight of the monarchy.

Our *anima* and *animus* are not stagnant; they evolve as we evolve. Anyone who has grown in their emotional, mental, and spiritual maturity will not personally relate with solely one archetype or be wholly satisfied with an immature expression of any of the archetypes in a partner.

Projection

Finding someone who mirrors the *anima* or *animus* is the result of what depth psychology calls "projection." Projection, like a movie projector, casts an inner psychological image onto the outer reality. The pictures we project onto others can contain either positive or negative traits. Usually there is some likeness in the outer personality to our projection. The person is matching up in ways to our inner image. All of us project to some extent; it's how we learn to understand and navigate life. We naturally identify what we meet in the present with our experiences from the past.

We can also discover a lot about the archetypes that we ourselves embody. What goddesses or gods resonate with you? Which archetypal figures feel familiar? Do their stories feel familiar? Jean Shinoda Bolen's books, *Gods in Every Man* and *Goddesses in Every Woman,* are excellent resources to discover, in mythic allegory, your own story, as well as the stories you are drawn to in a mate.

Once you discover the archetypal personalities, if you are not happy with your romantic past, you might be tempted to choose someone who bears no resemblance to the negative aspects of your *anima* or *animus* archetype, for example: if you have been drawn to 'Aphrodites," you will assiduously avoid them for fear of a femme fatale. If you have experienced abusive men, you will steer clear of the Zeus archetype, fearing you will attract another "despotic king."

In fact, this is not the solution. The better solution lies in incorporating a healthy expression of the archetype in your choice of partner, for example: the healthy, empathic Aphrodite, or just and fair Zeus. In the example given above, a woman may choose a poetic man with the capacity for leadership blending the best of both Zeus and the romantic poet of the Orpheus archetypes. In so doing, she brings into balance the masculine that was partially but not wholly embodied by her inherited masculine archetype. In other words, look for the balanced, healthy expression of that which lives within and calls you, as well as develop some aspect of those desirable traits in yourself. When you strive to grow in yourself some of the better characteristics of your mate, you become more whole.

The Creative Inspiration and Potential of the *Anima* and *Animus*

Jung noted that meeting someone who mirrors the internal figure of our *anima* or *animus* can powerfully lead to our own individuation whether or not that relationship finds fulfillment. Meeting that special person can enliven the inner muse, igniting a creative fire within us. Dante Alighieri's only meeting with Beatrice on a street in Florence inspired his *Divine Comedy*, a monumental contribution to literature. Beatrice, as his *anima*, reflected the feminine in his own soul, sparking an inner marriage, leading to the creation of his masterpiece, the literary child of that encounter.

Anima and *animus* can act as "psychopomps," guides of the soul. There are many examples of the inspiration that can be ignited by a female or male muse. My own book, *Alchemy of the Heart*, was initially inspired by my first love who activated in me the archetype of Dionysos. By finding a way to develop and integrate the best qualities of the *anima* or *animus* we become more whole. In this way, we grow through the process of falling in love with the "Other."

To whom have I been attracted during these years?

_____

_____

_____

_____

_____

_____

If I fell in love during these decades, what felt special about this person? (You may have fallen in love with your partner or with someone unattainable). Why did they attract me?

_____

_____

_____

_____

_____

_____

What did I learn about myself through that attraction?

_____

_____

_____

_____

_____

_____

If I committed to a partner, how did they reflect who I was at the time of the commitment? Were they what I was looking for consciously or unconsciously? How so?

_____

_____

_____

_____

_____

_____

_____

_____

Did my attractions change over these two decades? What does that tell me about how I changed?

_____

_____

_____

_____

_____

_____

Did any of these attractions (or ones in my teens or twenties) ignite my creativity? How so?

_____

_____

_____

_____

_____

_____

Returning to Early Wounds

Can I find any reflection of my early wounds reenacted through the course of my long-term relationships?

Examples might include being attracted to and committing to a person with whom you experience the same difficult feelings you had growing up with an elusive or abusive parent. A person we meet may seem familiar (i.e., like family) because of this resonance. But familiar may not mean that person is good for us or to us.

First, write the strongest uncomfortable quality you experienced with each of your parents. Then list the meaningful romantic relationships in your life and assign them to the best matching trait.

Are there any enduring memories and/or patterns of neglect, shame, abandonment, or abuse?

When I felt hurt as a child by my father, it felt like he (misjudged me, didn't value me, scared me, wasn't safe, etc.):

_____

_____

_____

_____

When I felt hurt by my mother, it felt like she (misjudged me, didn't value me, scared me, wasn't safe, etc.):

_____

_____

_____

_____

Now list your longer-term partners and consider whether you experienced anything similar.

_____

_____

_____

_____

_____

_____

_____

What qualities might I have been projecting onto my partners that seemed to drop away the longer we were together?

Both can be true (i.e., the person did change, and you had been projecting qualities onto them).

_____

_____

_____

_____

_____

_____

Have I been able to incorporate some of my partners' positive attributes and those positive projections into my own life?

Examples might include integrating a partner's self-confidence, attention to detail, patience, leadership qualities, ease of self-expression, etc.

_____

_____

_____

_____

_____

_____

List negative traits here:

_____

_____

_____

_____

_____

_____

Have I been able to transform the *prima materia* of their negative traits into positive expressions in my own life?

A partner's narcissism might get you to finally give attention to your own legitimate needs and self-love, or their verbal/emotional abuse might activate your ability to set boundaries and reclaim healthy power. You may be able to change the dynamic and stay in the partnership. If not, you may need to consider a change. In either case, their bad or simply irritating behavior can activate your own growth and integration. That said, physical abuse is never acceptable. Get help to get out ASAP.

_____

_____

_____

_____

_____

_____

If a relationship didn't last, were we able to end in a way that honored what had been between us? If not, how do I feel about that?

_____

_____

_____

_____

_____

If I chose to marry during this time in my life, what were my hopes for the marriage? How did I envision my future with this person (or persons, if you married more than once)?

_____

_____

_____

_____

_____

_____

_____

_____

Did my vision for the future shift and change as time went on, or did that vision come to pass?

_____

_____

_____

_____

_____

_____

Do I feel like I made the right choice to marry or not? Why? Did I grow from this partnership? If so, how?

This answer might be more complex than a simple yes or no. Explore all sides of your answer from the vantage point of when you made the choice, as well as from your present perspective of the decision. Maybe you feel that the children you had with this person, or the creative projects that resulted from your relationship, made your choice worthwhile.

_____

_____

_____

_____

_____

_____

_____

_____

Do/did I have others in my life with whom I can pursue interests not shared by my partner?

As no one person can fulfill all of our needs, consider the friends and extended community who have added to your life in ways your partner couldn't.

_____

_____

_____

_____

_____

Have any of my relationships as an adult served as corrective experiences for earlier wounds? If so, with whom, and how did that experience/healing occur?

Examples might include finally feeling heard, cherished, respected, and safe, in contrast to your earlier life experiences. Those corrective experiences might also have initiated the healing of an addiction that masked your deeper needs to feel loved, supported, and safe.

_____

_____

_____

_____

_____

How Trauma Impacts Our Responses

We have all been born into a traumatized world to varying degrees. The possible reactions we instinctively choose to manage this trauma are fight, flight, freeze, or fawn (a fourth trauma response that's used to pacify an abuser). One of these tends to be our go-to when faced with challenges that threaten our security or sense of safety.

Jews in hiding during the Holocaust or Indigenous children hiding from government agents bent on taking them away from their families and putting them into boarding schools are good examples of large-scale traumas that evoke these lifesaving reactions. Playing possum at such moments can make the difference between life and death or freedom and captivity. Likewise, puffing oneself up physically and making a racket can scare away a powerful predator. Running out of the way of an oncoming bus makes sense too.

However, as Peter Levine pointed out in his classic, *Waking the Tiger: Healing Trauma*, humans rarely shake off threats and move on like animals do in the wild. We tend to carry our trauma response, physically and psychically, far beyond the event. Add to this a predisposition to certain psychic and mental health difficulties via genetics, and we are programmed to live a great deal of our lives from this traumatic reactivity. This is hardly the best recipe for healthy interpersonal relationships.

Depending on both our nature and our nurture, we will puff ourselves up to meet a suspected threat or we will become small or even disappear by fleeing the situation. The third option is to leave the situation psychically through freezing, becoming practically immobile, the "deer in the headlights" instinct. Another person can hardly get a word out of us when we're frozen in this way because the mind has slowed way down to nearly a standstill. And, finally, there's the option of pacifying the threat through fawning, losing our dignity in the process. Identifying our go-to reaction is the first crucial step toward understanding and healing our trauma response.

Consider how you meet negativity in your environment. What is your instinctive reaction?

When I feel uncomfortable, or worse, threatened, I tend to _____
_____.

The problem arises when we utilize these tactics from a weak sense of self, having never learned how to constructively and respectfully dialogue through a disagreement. When we don't feel self-worth, or feel safe in the world, we are easily threatened and triggered by our surroundings and any potential conflict. How often have you used these survival tactics when there have been no dire threats? Have you questioned your response?

To varying degrees, each of these maneuvers in ordinary conflicts are a form of abandonment and betrayal of the self and the other. Relationships that might have grown to be more fulfilling have been damaged by our trauma responses, at times beyond repair. Most importantly, trauma responses push us toward self-abandonment, away from the potential for healing connection.

The first goal is acknowledgement—learning to notice your habitual patterns and then making the decision to practice staying present despite the impulse to act out our trauma response. If you need a time-out to regulate your nervous system and gather your thoughts, take it. That is good self-care. But be sure to let the other know how long you intend to leave the situation and when you will return to process. Simply leaving can trigger your partner's abandonment and further ignite their trauma response. This is just wasted time in finding a resolution that suits both of you.

Instead of "powering over," or hiding, can you begin to practice a feeling of being rooted in your sovereign self, without trying to dominate the conversation? Like a strong and sturdy tree, can you stand your ground while remaining flexible in the wind? This does not mean repressing or suppressing your thoughts and feelings. Rather, you strive to communicate in a way that respects both yourself and the other.

Healing our trauma reactions is a significant step in consciousness, healing ourselves, our relationships, and our world.

Sometimes Relationships Dissolve If They Don't Evolve

A lifelong partnership is a great blessing if, despite life's ups and downs, and expected periods of lull, it remains vital and creative. However, not every relationship is destined to last a lifetime. As the human lifespan has greatly increased and cultural and religious mores have become less punitive, many relationships dissolve if they don't evolve. This does not mean the relationship was a failure, nor the people in them. It can mean that either one or both people have simply grown in different directions, and the partnership is no longer constructive and creative.

If a relationship becomes destructive without one or both partners willing to change, it is definitely time to get out. Maybe, in the past, you tended to attract or be drawn to people who were either abusive, smothering, or elusive (or any combination) because of the similarity with your upbringing. Another name for this is "trauma bonding." We feel comfortable with the discomfort because it is so familiar. It literally feels like being with family. But familiar might be destructive.

Below, write how you have changed and grown in terms of the people whom you attract or who you choose as partners. Notice how you have worked with the *prima materia*, and evolved.

How have I changed in terms of how I approach relationships? What do I know now about my needs and desires?

_____

_____

_____

_____

_____

_____

_____

_____

A Broken Heart—The Wounding of Humiliation

As poet David Whyte points out, we have each suffered humiliation and shame in some way. Humiliation can come in the form of a broken heart, getting fired from a job, an unwanted divorce, rejection by a religious community or family, etc. When that humiliation occurs in adulthood, we have the choice to either mask the wound or see it as an invitation into greater maturity and depth. Making the choice to dive in calls for great courage. The way through the pain of humiliation is to stay with that pain consciously, letting it ripen the soul. Eventually, we find integration and relief, but not through the quick fix of denial or identifying as a victim.

> Humiliation has that beautiful root of humilis, meaning ground or soil. It is both the ground that you come to and the soil from which the new harvest is grown. On every path you take in life, whether it's an intimate relationship, the relationship to a child, the relationship to your work and vocation, or the relationship to yourself, you will have your heart broken.[1]

1. David Whyte on *Welcoming Humiliation*, *The Daily Good*, in conversation with Lindy Alexander, Syndicated from dumbofeather.com, May 23, 2018.

Have We Met Before?

It is estimated that more than half the world's population believes in reincarnation. In contrast to Western culture, most Eastern cultures and religions, as well as many worldwide indigenous traditions, take the idea of reincarnation for granted as it matches what we see in nature. Nature is cyclic, not linear. Thus, if birth is a doorway into this dimension, death is a doorway into another dimension, and there is a vast cycle of return. Life doesn't end; it simply transmutes into new forms and possibly renews itself in other embodiments.

If reincarnation is part of your belief system, did you have an intuition, knowing your connection with these lovers and deeper friendships? If so, what did you imagine about that connection?

It is absolutely fine to use your imagination here. Even if such pictures or feelings are purely imaginal, they still hold information about our perceptions of the other and color our responses and expectations.

Friends and Lovers

_____

_____

_____

_____

_____

_____

_____

_____

_____

_____

What do I feel/know is the purpose, or purposes, of our relationship?

_____

_____

_____

_____

_____

_____

_____

Letting Go

Imagining myself as a screenwriter, how might I write a positive conclusion to my experiences of loss and grief in my relationships?

Write an ending that honors both of you, allowing each of you freedom and freewill. This exercise is useful for both formulating how you might handle endings with others in the future and giving your subconscious a healing alternative.

_____

_____

_____

_____

_____

_____

_____

_____

Relationships: Parenthood

Even if you are not currently a parent, this section may be useful if you are considering parenthood in the future.

Who are my children?

These can be biological, step, or foster children.

_____

_____

_____

_____

_____

_____

How do I feel about being a parent?

_____

_____

_____

_____

Does parenting seem to come naturally to me or not? If not, how do I address that?

_____

_____

_____

_____

_____

1. medlineplus.gov.

How do I see my job as a parent? What do I believe is most important for me to do and achieve as a parent?

_____

_____

_____

_____

The theory of nurture versus nature is ongoing. In Greece, approximately 400 years before the common era, philosophers Plato and Aristotle were pondering this question. Plato taught that the soul brings knowledge and tendencies (nature) into our physical incarnation, while Aristotle believed we know nothing until experience informs us (nurture).

The science of genetics began in the 1800s with the work of Gregor Mendel. It proved that we inherit our physical traits and tendencies. Genetic scientists today estimate that we inherit 20 to 60 percent of our temperament as well.[1]

A metaphysical perspective of nature versus nurture suggests that a soul gravitates toward the best set of physical and environmental circumstances for its needs and goals. This explanation seeks to mediate between the purely scientific and the purely spiritual points of view, and between Aristotle's and Plato's perspectives.

The importance of nature and nurture are both valid and valuable. However, parenting tends to reveal where we fall on the side of nature versus nurture. We tend to favor or find evidence for one over the other, depending on our perspective. The following question explores this difference.

Do I see my children as mostly having their own intrinsic natures awaiting discovery and nurture, or do I see my children as malleable and shaped primarily by the experiences and teachings I give them?

_____

_____

_____

_____

_____

The next series of questions focus on our parents' values and our own, what we want to pass on generationally, and what we would like to change moving forward.

How are my parenting goals the same as or different from what I believe my own parents' goals were with me?

_____

_____

_____

_____

_____

_____

How are my values the same as each of my parents' values, and how are they different?

My mother placed high value on:

_____

_____

_____

_____

My father placed high value on:

_____

_____

_____

_____

My own values are like my parents' values in these ways:

_____

_____

_____

_____

_____

_____

My values differ from my parents' values in these ways:

_____

_____

_____

_____

_____

How would I like my own parenting to be like my parents' approach?

_____

_____

_____

_____

How would I like it to be different?

_____

_____

_____

_____

Do I see myself as more of a hands-on or hands-off parent? How much involvement and control do I feel is best?

_____

_____

_____

_____

If I see myself as a hands-on parent, is this approach motivated primarily by a healthy sense of responsibility or does it stem from fear (or maybe a mixture of both)? If fear is a primary motive behind my parenting approach, what is it that I'm afraid of? Is my fear justified with my child's current circumstances?

If I am a mostly hands-off parent, why? Was I overcontrolled as a child? Am I afraid to know what my child might be up to, or do I have a healthy sense of trust in their development (or maybe a mixture of both)?

_____

_____

_____

_____

_____

It is interesting to explore the weight and validity of our fear, and to what extent it imposes on our parenting. How much of our fear is rational? There are so many factors to consider: bullies at school, the neighborhood we live in, the race and ethnicity of our children, their gender expression and sexuality, religious beliefs and practices—all of these and so many more play a part in how we navigate the line between fear and protection as parents. Lack of legitimate caution can be a form of neglect.

But if your children are in a relatively safe position, how much of your fear is inherited and exaggerated? Over control of children can be equally as damaging as neglect, not only to their self-esteem and developing sense of autonomy, but also to their creativity. In the lines below, reflect on these issues.

_____

_____

_____

_____

_____

_____

_____

How does my parenting style reflect my experience growing up with my parents? Did I experience their trust, or did I experience their fears? How much do I tend toward the other end of the spectrum in my parenting approach?

_____

_____

_____

_____

_____

_____

Discipline

Esoteric spiritual traditions teach that love and power, when balanced, produce wisdom. Power without love is cruelty, while love without power is weakness. Our journey through life is an ongoing process of learning how to weave love and power together in healthy balance. Parenting offers us a potent opportunity to exercise balanced love and power, and, in doing so, developing and demonstrating true wisdom.

What are my beliefs about discipline? How do I discipline my children, and what do I see as its purpose? What do I want to teach them through my methods of discipline?

_____

_____

_____

_____

_____

_____

Do I exercise my responsibility as a parent in a way that supports the growth of my children rather than intimidates and dominates? Do I exercise my role as a parent in a way that instructs and empowers my children rather than overpowers/ disempowers them? If not, why?

_____

_____

_____

_____

_____

_____

Can I think of ways to repair our relationship, if needed?

_____

_____

_____

_____

Do I value the growing sense of self-trust and independence I see developing in my children? Are these goals evident in my parenting? If not enough, how can I promote these values?

This question is still a valid one if you now have grown children and are in relationship with them.

_____

_____

_____

_____

_____

_____

Have I modeled responsibility to others, to community, and for themselves?

_____

_____

More than anything we say to them, children learn by example. Of course, there are always times we aren't perfect models. And there are children who fail to learn by our example. But do we have teaching by example as an ideal?

Do I practice what I preach with my children? For example, if I insist they have clean language, do I swear? Am I a good model to my children? Could I be better? How?

_____

_____

_____

_____

_____

_____

_____

_____

_____

Have I learned and modeled good communication skills?

_____

_____

_____

_____

If my children are still growing, are there more ways that I can be actively present, giving them clear boundaries that support their growth and safety?

_____
_____
_____
_____
_____

How am I encouraging a sense of mutual trust?

Note: If your children keep a journal, do not invade their privacy. This may be the only place they have to work out their feelings without fear. If you need answers, find another way. Your children's earned trust will pay off. They will be far more likely to confide in you if they know they can trust you.

_____
_____
_____
_____
_____

Do I feel I see and appreciate my children's unique selves as well as their gifts?

This question is the most important one in this section. Your children will feel whether you respect their intrinsic nature. This seeing goes a long way in establishing a lifelong relationship of mutual care and respect.

_____
_____
_____
_____
_____

"Soul respect," as Khalil Gibran writes about it in *The Prophet*, is a crucial element in parenting. If a child feels seen and valued for who they are, as well as feeling a sense of trust and safety, chances are high that they will grow into an adult with self-worth who makes healthy choices.

In *The Prophet* he writes,

Your children are not your children. They are the sons and daughters of Life's longing for itself. They come through you but not from you. And though they are with you yet they belong not to you.

You may give them your love but not your thoughts,

For they have their own thoughts.

You may house their bodies but not their souls,

For their souls dwell in the house of tomorrow, which you cannot visit, not even in your dreams.

You may strive to be like them, but seek not to make them like you.

For life goes not backward nor tarries with yesterday.

You are the bows from which your children as living arrows are sent forth.

The archer sees the mark upon the path of the infinite, and He bends you with His might that

His arrows might go swift and far. Let your bending in the archer's hand be for gladness;

For even as He loves the arrow that flies, so He loves also the bow that is stable.[2]

Did I feel seen and honored by my own parents in this way?

_____

_____

_____

_____

2. Gibran, Khalil. "On Children," *The Prophet*, Alfred A. Knopf, 1923.

Do my children feel genuinely honored by me for who they are? Though I may appreciate their successes, am I able to separate these from their essential value and from my own? Do my children know they are respected at their core (a "soul respect") by me? If not, how can I change and help heal this?

_____

_____

_____

_____

_____

_____

_____

_____

_____

Exploring Our Different Parenting Styles

Does my partner or co-parent have the same philosophy and style of parenting as I do? If not, how do we differ?

_____

_____

_____

_____

_____

If our parenting styles are different, what are the pros and cons of these differences? Are we complementary or oppositional in our differences?

_____

_____

_____

_____

_____

_____

Is it possible to find the positive contributions that my co-parent offers? If so what are they?

Finding what the other parent offers and respecting these offerings can go a long way toward more effective co-parenting and establishing a sense of safety in your child's world.

_____

_____

_____

_____

_____

_____

What do we agree on in terms of our children and our vision for them? How can I support that vision, both personally and in conversation with my partner/co-parent?

_____

_____

_____

_____

When we are the best version of ourselves as parents, who are we? What do we each uniquely contribute?

_____

_____

_____

_____

In cases of separation and divorce, the trust between parents may be severely damaged. As a result, co-parenting can be especially difficult. It is helpful to consider the possibility of soul choices and soul contracts on the part of your children in relationship to parents. These choices are not made by the *personality* of the child but rather by their soul. It is based on the idea that one lifetime isn't enough to fully develop a human being psychologically or spiritually. The soul agrees to a certain context beforehand that offers the desired opportunities for its future growth and service.

Whether or not you have a spiritual perspective, there are countless stories of individuals who have taken extraordinarily difficult childhood experiences and transformed those woundings into gifts they offer to the world, finding greater depth and wholeness within themselves in the process. While we want to make our children's lives as positive as we can, they may ultimately find growth in the experience of struggle. We must make difficult choices at times to create the best foundation possible for them, but sometimes there is no ideal solution.

When we have done all we're able to do to deter their suffering, our children may ultimately find a way to deepen and grow through difficult circumstances.

Conflicting Styles of Parenting

As mentioned earlier in the discussion about nature versus nurture, a common difficulty in the situation of conflicting parenting styles is the tendency of each parent to compensate for the other's style. One parent may feel the other is too strict and punitive, while the other may feel the child is too coddled and indulged. This split in perspective, not uncommon, leads to an extreme and out of balance environment for children. The children typically learn quickly who will give them what they want and who won't. This creates a good guy/bad guy dynamic, splitting the parents and upending a cohesive, healthy structure on which the children can rely for their stability. The following question considers the possibility (or impossibility) of finding common ground and respect for one another's perspectives and concerns.

Where our views of parenting are oppositional, can I envision how we might more constructively support one another, honoring our differing gifts and approaches? What might that look like?

_____

_____

_____

_____

_____

_____

_____

_____

_____

_____

A Note on Divorce and Children

Supportive co-parenting is the most important goal whether you are married, separated, or divorced. Some of my clients have stayed together for the sake of the children and others have left the marriage for the sake of themselves and the children. Both paths can be fraught with pain and conflict and be difficult to navigate from a parenting perspective. Children are exquisitely sensitive to the emotional temperature in the home. Marriages that are rife with resentment, anger, sorrow, or fear, are rarely, if ever, entirely invisible to the child. Couples counseling to heal, if possible, the damaged relationship is the first step.

If the marriage is beyond repair, the couple may decide on separation and divorce. This is never easy when parenting is involved. Acting as respectful collaborators in raising their children is *the* most important goal of separated and divorced parents. When children are used as a weapon against the other parent, or as a go-between in parental concerns, this leaves a lasting and damaging mark. Parenting classes, co-parenting therapy sessions, and workshops are very helpful in educating parents and resolving these difficulties.

When a peaceable co-parenting situation simply isn't possible, if at least one parent offers a genuinely peaceful, safe, and supportive environment, the children will likely thrive. Ultimately, a child will feel most loved and safe when there is as much real peace and security as possible, and when it's clear what is expected of them.

Dealing with Stress

Parenting, though an opportunity for great joy, can easily elevate the stress levels in each parent. As mentioned earlier, four reactions have been noted in high stress situations: fight, flight, freeze, and fawn. We tend to unconsciously pick one of these as our go-to when we are under too much stress. Fawning in this case looks like pacifying the child too easily and too often by giving in to their demands.

How do I tend to react in high-stress parenting situations? Do I get angry, do I leave the situation (and if so, how?), do I slow down to near-paralysis emotionally and mentally, or do I typically buy a toy or treat to quiet my child?

_____

_____

_____

_____

Reacting is different from *responding*. Reacting is reflexive, without considered thought. Responding uses the prefrontal cortex and its cognitive process, it is more than instinctive. Instinct is extremely useful in near-death encounters but not usually adequate, and often destructive, in navigating interpersonal relationships.

Our goal, especially in parenting, is to *respond* to our children. When we pause to catch our breath and think through the most effective way to move forward, we calm our nervous system and gain greater clarity and choice in how we want to handle the situation. In doing so, we model maturity.

How is my reaction the same or different from my parents/caregivers growing up? How did my mother and my father individually react to high stress? Who am I most like? How am I different?

_____

_____

_____

_____

What choices have I made in how I manage stress in parenting? How do I take care of myself?

Some examples of positive self-management and self-care include time-outs for yourself (communicating a specified limit to your child so as not to provoke feelings of abandonment), taking at least three deep breaths before responding to a situation, journaling, walking and exercise, time in nature, baths, massage, calling a trusted friend, etc. Refer to your self-care, reset list to see more ways you can care for yourself in high-stress parenting situations.

You can also use these methods to help your children with stress. Nature, baths, massage, yoga, journaling, learning to take breaths, and music all help to shift and stabilize mood.

_____

_____

_____

_____

Self-Care

Do I practice ongoing self-care? How is my overall health? What is my body telling me about my self-care practices (or lack thereof)? Do I take the time to restore and replenish? How could I better honor my body and its needs?

A stressed-out parent creates stress in the child. Doing your best to take care of yourself is a gift to your child. Modeling healthy self-care is a positive value you can teach your children through example.

_____

_____

_____

_____

How do or can I cultivate my own interests and grow as a person while being a parent and a partner or co-parent?

_____

_____

_____

_____

_____

Considering the best aspects of my own parents, which qualities have I incorporated into my own life and given to the next generation through example and teaching?

_____

_____

_____

_____

_____

_____

_____

_____

How do I hope to have enriched the lives of my child/children? What values and resources, both material and spiritual, do I hope to give them?

_____

_____

_____

_____

_____

If my child/children's decisions turn out to be different than the ones I would make, both personally and professionally, how do I feel about this? What could and couldn't I accept easily and why?

A difference in choice might include who they choose as a partner, what they choose as a profession or their religion, their politics, sexuality and gender identity, where to live (urban, rural, abroad), being intentionally single, deciding not to have children, etc.

_____

_____

_____

_____

_____

_____

Why are these differences difficult for me to accept?

_____

_____

_____

_____

Can I imagine myself accepting these differences? If not, is it possible to reach a level of tolerance if their choices do not actually physically harm themselves or another?

A way to imagine the value for us in finding acceptance of these differences is to see them as a widening of our heart's capacity to love. This can be especially difficult when our own identity and heritage feel threatened. Working internally with these possible threats to our expectations can help.

_____

_____

_____

_____

How do I hope to be seen and experienced by my child/children at the end of my life? What do I hope for in terms of our relationship?

_____

_____

_____

_____

Is there anything I can do now as well as in the future to promote that outcome?

_____

_____

_____

_____

As a result of the parenting experience, how have I grown psychologically and spiritually? What still needs work? What has parenting taught me about my gifts, as well as the qualities that need strengthening?

_____

_____

_____

_____

_____

_____

_____

_____

_____

_____

_____

What has my own experience of parenting revealed to me about my own parents (their challenges, struggles, their missteps, and their successes as parents)?

_____

_____

_____

_____

What have I learned from my children?

_____

_____

_____

_____

_____

_____

_____

_____

_____

Living a Symbolic Life—The World as Your House of Mirrors

The people in our lives, like mirrors, help us see parts of ourselves that we may be blind to, parts that are alive and well underneath the surface layer of our consciousness. When we see positive reflections in the situations and people we attract, these mirrors reflect ways in which we are healthy or have grown.

They can also reveal our inner distortions and places in ourselves we need to tend and heal.

Often, they hold qualities that we have done our best to push away. They reveal the next shadow work calling us. They prompt us to ask ourselves more questions. What in us has been activated and why? Is there an event or person from the past mirrored in this new person or situation? If we are judging that person, making them bad or wrong, can we move to the more neutral stance of discernment, a more objective perception? What belief about ourselves is being called into question? This is a slight but monumental shift in consciousness. We see what they triggered from our past. We extricate them from the hook to that memory, and see them now, warts and all, with compassion. We work with our own material. We may still decide to distance ourselves from someone who has hurt us or others, but we are doing so with conscious awareness.

Situations also arise that mirror our inner work. Maybe we have an accident. Maybe the accident was really no accident. In my experience, there are no accidents. Whatever happens is there as a possible instruction and maybe an outright gift. Maybe the event called our attention to the emotional and mental changes we needed to make at the time, or to a service we felt called to do but hadn't made time for. Maybe we just need to slow down.

Maybe the other person involved in the accident needed some compassion. I was once in a car collision in which no one was hurt but the other woman had just come from holding the body of her dead elderly mother. She was upset and she needed connection. The negative connection of our car accident became a moment of positive connection and healing.

Maybe the accident will call us to a bigger life with more meaning. I know more than one person for whom a devastating accident dramatically changed the course of life. It allowed them to leave an unproductive path and find their calling. At the point of a severe crisis, a person is challenged to rethink their life and its direction. Meaning can be excavated from the debris of loss.

Bodily symptoms, too, hold information and potential. Knees give out, ankles break, backs ache. Perhaps we have been moving forward too quickly without giving due attention to processes like grief or anger. Maybe we need to slow down and find connection rather than running past life's offerings.

Shadow Work and Your Values

You have considered the shadow qualities in your parents and possibly your siblings; now it is time to extend that review to friends and lovers who are or have been in your life. The longevity of our relationships greatly depends on sharing similar values. A way to get clear on your nonnegotiable values is to reflect on why you may have ended relationships in the past.

In the spaces below, write the person's name and what caused you to distance or end the relationship as it had been. Next, clarify what *value* felt violated in that relationship (loyalty, empathy, safety, respect, freedom, etc.).

_____

_____

_____

_____

_____

_____

_____

_____

_____

Knowing who you are and what is important to you empowers you to make better relationship choices in the future.

Now cast a wider net for this exploration.

What qualities and attitudes trigger me in strangers? Why? What value am I protecting?

An example might be feeling anger triggered in you when you see someone smoking in public. The underlying values you're protecting might be consideration of others, respect for others, and health.

In the following exercise you are asked to consider four examples of times you are triggered, leading to you forming a judgment of the other person.

Fill out the first two lines, but leave the third line (the hidden nugget of value) blank for now.

1) It really bothers me when people _____

The value I am protecting is _____

(Do **not** answer the following question until you finish answering all four of the initial two questions.)

The hidden nugget of value in their misbehavior might be: _____

2) It really bothers me when people _____

The value I am protecting is _____

(Do **not** answer the following question until you finish answering all four of the initial two questions.)

The hidden nugget of value in their misbehavior might be: _____

3) It really bothers me when people _____

The value I am protecting is _____

(Do **not** answer the following question until you finish answering all four of the initial two questions.)

The hidden nugget of value in their misbehavior might be: _____

4) It really bothers me when people _____

The value I am protecting is _____

(Do **not** answer the following question until you finish answering all four of the initial questions.)

The hidden nugget of value in their misbehavior might be: _____

Before you answer the last question of the four questions read this:

Earlier, we looked at negative qualities in our parents and excavated the potential in those qualities for our own enrichment. We can do the same practice for the negative expressions that trigger us in others. We do not have to disown or stop protecting our values, but we can include what might be a positive, life-enhancing attribute into our lives that may be currently distorted and hiding in a negative expression.

Consider how whatever unwelcome behavior could be reframed or modified to a more positive expression. What might that be? Would possessing the *positive* aspect of that quality enrich your own life? Can you imagine standing for your values, while adding an appreciation for the hidden value within the distorted expressions we see in others?

Here are some examples of this transformative potential:

*A grandstanding, braggart politician could hold the seed of *self-confidence*.

*A smoker could stand for *freedom*, though that value has been distorted into unhealthful and disrespectful behavior.

*An alcoholic, though exhibiting an unhealthy distortion, could stand for the value of *releasing rigid control and inhibitions or be a call to spirit rather than spirits*. We might also consider in what ways we ourselves may be acting out addictions. An excessive concern of any kind points to addiction.

This exercise extends your own potential as you retrieve the disowned parts being expressed in a distorted manner by others. It also enhances your discernment and compassion. Discernment is a neutral evaluation in contrast to judgment, which so often too harshly creates division and separation. Compassion is the understanding that, as humans, we are all struggling in some manner.

Now go back to the exercise above and fill in the last line, assigning the triggering behaviors you listed with the *positive values* each might be concealing.

Questioning Our Inhibiting Beliefs

We have already explored the possible negative beliefs we may have in regard to money. Here are some other areas where negative beliefs could be holding us back. Many, if not most of us, carry conscious and subconscious beliefs. The subconscious is extremely powerful. Left to its own devices, it can severely block our happiness and fulfillment. Reprogramming these beliefs in a healthy way supports our efforts and our success.

We have already explored the possibly inhibiting beliefs we have about money. Here are some other beliefs that may be holding us back from what we could have and achieve in life:

Some distorted beliefs include:

1) Everyone knows more than I do.
2) The world is dangerous.
3) I am only safe when I am alone.
4) Men (and/or women) are not to be trusted.
5) People are difficult.
6) I must win at any cost. "The ends justify the means."
7) Why am I always the victim?
8) Everything has been done before, so why try?
9) I am an outsider. No one understands me.
10) When is it *my* turn?
11) No one will ever love me just for me.
12) Vulnerability is dangerous.
13) The artist has a hard life.
14) Love (or success) isn't in the cards for me.
15) There's never enough time.
16) Life is hard.
17) I am too _____... No one will want me.
18) If I am generous (with my time, money, expertise)...I will be poor.
19) People always take advantage of the nice guy.
20) It's a dog eat dog world.

Circle the ones that feel true to you. Can you think of any others?

_____

_____

_____

_____

_____

_____

_____

_____

_____

_____

Many of our life circumstances are a result of these embedded beliefs. Generally, people are attracted to a positive person. Positive people are far more likely to receive support and, as a result, achieve success in life more regularly than negative, hopeless people.

By doing this alchemizing work, you are turning negatives into positives and rough stones into gems. A vital step in owning your mastery as an alchemist is dismantling the inhibitions that prevent you from experiencing joy and success. This world needs joy, not empty distraction, and it needs success, not disillusionment and settling. You get to choose.

Write alternative beliefs that cancel out the negative ones you circled (as well as the ones you added):

_____

_____

_____

_____

_____

_____

_____

_____

_____

_____

_____

_____

_____

In questioning these beliefs, your subconscious will begin to soften its walls of defense, allowing for the possibility of a happier and more fulfilled life. Daily affirming new positive beliefs, while supporting them with positive action, dislodges and ultimately dissolves old restrictive patterns.

Make New Agreements

Don Miguel Ruiz, in his powerful book, *The Four Agreements*, outlines four positive cornerstone beliefs we can adopt to replace the many negative ones we've consciously or unconsciously accepted since childhood.

1) Be impeccable in your word.

Not only does this mean that you follow through on what you say you'll do, it also applies to how we speak about others and to ourselves. Do we speak in unkind terms? He calls this unkindness "black magic." Figuratively, we are casting negative spells on ourselves and on others through our negative thoughts and words.

2) Do not take anything personally.

Big challenge! When you achieve this, you experience true freedom! It's an ongoing practice.

3) Do not make assumptions.

In other words, don't assume what others are thinking or their motives.

4) Always do your best.

We can't do more than that.

Every success begins with a positive belief about ourselves and what is possible. Your negative beliefs have been black magic used against yourself and others. Be the magician you are born to be and cast spells of positive magic for yourself and others.

Boundaries

How am I in terms of healthy boundaries?

Healthy boundaries support our intentions and respect our needs and those of others. Good boundaries go hand-in-hand with healthy self-esteem (neither an inflated sense of superiority nor a deflated sense of unworthiness). As you honor your unique beauty and worth, so, too, do you take care of your own emotional psychic and physical space.

_____
_____
_____
_____
_____
_____

How can I improve my boundaries if they are not as good as they could be?

_____
_____
_____
_____

If my boundaries are too self-protective (often as a result of experiences that created inhibiting beliefs), how could I start to create some openings for new experiences?

_____
_____
_____
_____
_____

Spirituality and Values

How would I define my spirituality during this time in my life?

_____

_____

_____

_____

Has my spirituality shifted during adulthood? If so, how, and in what ways?

_____

_____

_____

_____

_____

_____

How about my values? What are they, and have they remained basically the same or shifted as I've grown older?

_____

_____

_____

_____

Do I feel any conflict with religion, especially the religion in which I was raised? If so, how have I come to terms or not with that conflict?

_____

_____

_____

_____

If I left the religion of my upbringing or have a different expression of it than my family, has this shift created conflict? How have I navigated this? What qualities have I developed in navigating this difference, or do I feel weakened by that conflict?

_____

_____

_____

_____

_____

_____

If my spirituality has been criticized by family or community, have I been able to mourn the loss of connection? Have I found other sources of connection?

_____

_____

_____

_____

_____

_____

How are my values present in my political views?

_____

_____

_____

_____

Are my political views the same as or different from my partner's, my family's, my community's? If different, how so?

_____

_____

_____

_____

_____

_____

If I experience different perspectives and values regarding spirituality and politics from my partner, friends, family, or community, how do I navigate those differences in my relationships?

_____

_____

_____

_____

_____

_____

Peak Experiences

Have you ever had what Abraham Maslow termed a "peak experience"? In a peak experience, we feel a powerful sense of coherence and oneness, variously described as profound experiences of awe, reverence, humility, and bliss. These moments can be triggered by nature, art, sex, creative work, music, scientific revelation, introspection, and meditation. If you've had what feels like a peak experience, describe it in the space below.

_____

_____

_____

_____

_____

_____

_____

_____

Your Soul's Purpose and Your Life's Mission

The *Soul*, as I am defining it here, is what makes you *You*, regardless of your age. Though you are not the same person you were when you were a child, or the same person you were a decade or even a year ago, there is a part of you that transcends time.

The soul has also been equated with the larger and wiser part of each of us, larger and wiser than our ego and personality. If you believe in the theory of reincarnation, you can imagine your soul as the mothership for all the various personalities it has used to experience and evolution. Experience and evolution are the *soul's purpose* and goal.

Your *soul mission* refers to your service to humanity and the earth. Earlier we explored the idea of a calling. A calling is your soul's mission. It may look grand, or it may be largely invisible in the world. No matter, you have an impact simply by being here.

Some examples of a soul mission are nurturing others, healing the sick, fighting for justice, promoting freedom, protecting and serving others, caring for the earth, standing in and for a greater truth, creating beauty, making others laugh and feel uplifted, promoting peace, expanding limiting beliefs, and elevating consciousness.

If you are uncomfortable with the word soul, you can replace it with the Dialectic Behavioral Therapy concept of the wise mind.

Ask the part of yourself that has a more transpersonal view:

What can you tell me about the purpose behind the circumstances of my life? What opportunities were offered for my growth?

_____

_____

_____

_____

_____

_____

_____

_____

How am I doing in meeting the challenges and opportunities that have been offered to me for my own growth? Am I on track?

_____

_____

_____

_____

_____

_____

_____

_____

Do I have a soul mission? What is it?

Your mission may include one or more possible contributions to life.

_____

_____

_____

_____

_____

How can I best move forward in fulfilling more of my mission, as I understand it?

_____

_____

_____

_____
_____
_____
_____
_____
_____
_____

What do you want to tell me about my next level of growth?

_____
_____
_____
_____
_____
_____

What steps do I need to take to get there?

_____
_____
_____
_____
_____
_____
_____
_____
_____

228 Adulthood / THE ALCHEMY OF YOUR LIFE

Is there anything more you want to tell me at this time?

_____

_____

_____

_____

_____

You can do a more specific version of this exercise at any time. Lee Harris, an intuitive and psycho/spiritual guide, teaches people to contact their souls whenever they have a question about their experiences or their progress, or when they need to make an impactful choice.

The question he poses is, "What does my soul want to tell me today (or on this topic)?" This is a practical method for excavating wisdom on a deeper level. The practice of asking this question and deeply listening for and to an answer cultivates a greater independence from outside authorities, empowering us to be our best counsel. This is not frivolous work. Too often we hand over our power to outsiders, whether they are politicians, clergy, doctors, or other authorities. Likewise, we often make choices from our more surface-level consciousness. Consulting what Dialectical Behavioral Therapy calls our wise mind can bring about a deeper and more considered response to life.

We are living in a powerful period of dismantling of the old institutions on which we used to rely for answers. With ongoing revelations of corruption and conflicting narratives, we are invited to remove our idealistic projections of other people and institutions. While initially disorienting, the positive result of this breakdown is discovering answers that we can access directly, stepping into a more mature adulthood.

The ancient guru tradition of India teaches that the true guru resides within each of us. The Sanskrit meaning of the word guru means "remover of ignorance or darkness." The work you have done here, and the soul work you continue to do once you've completed this workbook, will strengthen your self-knowledge and personal sense of value and sovereignty. You will gradually polish the rough-hewn elements of your life to reveal the hidden gems.

Dream Work as Alchemy

What to Remember When Waking

In that first
hardly noticed
moment
in which you wake,
coming back
to this life
from the other
more secret,
moveable
and frighteningly
honest
world
where everything
began,
there is a small
opening
into the day
which closes
the moment
you begin
your plans.

What you can plan
is too small
for you to live.

What you can live
wholeheartedly
will make plans
enough
for the vitality
hidden in your sleep.

To become human
is to become visible
while carrying
what is hidden
as a gift to others.

To remember
the other world
in this world
is to live in your
true inheritance.

You are not
a troubled guest
on this earth,
you are not
an accident
amidst other accidents
you were invited
from another and greater
night
than the one
from which
you have just emerged.

Now, looking through
the slanting light
of the morning
window toward
the mountain
presence
of everything
that can be,
what urgency
calls you to your
one love? What shape
waits in the seed
of you to grow
and spread

its branches
against a future sky?

in the fertile sea?
In the trees
beyond the house?
In the life
you can imagine
for yourself?
In the open
and lovely
white page
on the waiting desk?[1]

The deeper psyche is always at work accumulating our experiences and trying to digest them. Some dreams are a simple processing of our day, and some work on the bigger issues in our lives, offering us clues as to where we need to put our focus and grow. They often give us information that lies below the surface of our conscious mind. Sometimes they present quite forcefully, and at other times more enigmatically.

Difficult to process material, especially in the case of trauma, shows up in repeated dream themes that demand our attention. Dr. W. Brugh Joy suggested that nightmares may be offering the dreamer the possibility of a breakthrough, letting us know we are ready to face our fears and our buried traumas.

Trauma can get us stuck in rumination, both consciously and unconsciously. But when we bring the light of our awareness and attention to the darkness, our dreams change, and healing begins to take place. Enlightenment is not transcending the darkness but rather bringing light to it.

There are dreams of affirmation, too, that communicate a sort of congratulations from our deeper psyche and mark the graduation of our evolution to a new level. Learning your own lexicon of symbols derived from your experiences—as well as having access to a good dictionary of symbols that document worldwide archetypal associations (what Jung called the Collective Unconscious) can be a wonderful, valuable, and intriguing path of self-discovery. Jung discovered symbols of the alchemical process reflected in the dreams of his clients, who had

---

1. David Whyte, *What to Remember When Waking*, from *David Whyte: Essentials*. © 2020 David Whyte. Reprinted with permission from David Whyte and Many Rivers Company, LLC, Langley, WA www.davidwhyte.com.

no conscious awareness of alchemy. This discovery actually served as proof to Jung that there was a larger evolutionary intention in our dreamlife and of the psyche itself.

We dream every night, but often we forget our dreams as we enter our conscious day life. Recording them, or simply jotting down the remembered fragments, invites more dream recovery into our experience. Many people also tend to dream more in the winter months, which is a naturally more inward-turning time.

It is useful to have some handy way to record your dreams beside your bed and to try recalling as much as possible before going about your day. Repeating the dream to yourself before you get up will help you recall it when you go to record it. You do not have to write your dreams down before you get up—I always get a morning coffee or tea first—but don't wait too long. If you wake from a dream in the middle of the night, just write or record the main elements while keeping the lights low. Wonderful information can come through even the most prosaic, ordinary-seeming dream, especially when we stay attuned to their symbols and messages. Dreams are our alchemizers.

Note: Before sleep, you can ask your psyche to provide the most meaningful dream just before you are due to wake in the morning. The psyche does often respond to this request. That way we get less interrupted sleep during the night and still have something valuable to work with when we wake.

Big Dreams and Visions

Native American traditions speak of the possibility of receiving a "Big Dream," that is, a dream that's extraordinarily vivid and unusual, carrying a sense of numinosity and otherworldly awe. These dreams bring insight into one's life mission, often leading us back to the road best suited to us. If you have experienced a "Big Dream," or more than one, write your experience below.

_____

_____

_____

_____

_____

_____

_____

_____

_____

_____

_____

_____

_____

_____

Visions, though rare, do occur. They are not normally visual in the sense that we see something outside of ourselves. More typically they occur in our mind's eye. Nevertheless, they have a lasting and profound effect. David Spangler, former codirector of the Findhorn Foundation and founder of the Lorian Foundation, records a life-changing vision he experienced as a young man, determining his life's direction, in his book *Apprenticed to Spirit; The Education of a Soul.*

If you have ever experienced an interior vision (or, far more rarely, an exterior one) that has had a life-changing impact, you are invited to record it here.

_____

_____

_____

_____

_____

_____

_____

_____

_____

_____

How did I understand the messages within this "Big Dream" dream, or vision? How did it affect my life moving forward?

This can be an invisible yet deeply felt effect that we carry with us moving forward.

_____

_____

_____

_____

_____

_____

_____

Synchronicities

A synchronicity is a meaningful, sometimes serendipitous, coincidence. Synchronicities can cause us to gasp in amazement, and usually they carry with them a feeling of affirmation or uncanny warning. They seem to be a type of communication from an invisible source, whether we call that spirit, soul, or the unconscious.

They are illogical, seemingly "acausal," but they make sense on a deep level. They can affect the course of our lives. They can also be overlooked or minimized in importance. If you've had a life-changing synchronicity or commonly experience them, record that here.

_____

_____

_____

_____

_____

_____

_____

What did these events mean to me? How did I interpret them?

_____

_____

_____

_____

_____

_____

_____

_____

What does my interpretation say about what I value?

_____

_____

_____

_____

The Context of our Lives—Our Relationship to Place

Just as people and events influence us and the course of our lives, so do places and spaces. We not only have relationships with people, but we are also constantly in relationship with our environment.

Where you were born and where you grew up might be different. You might have lived in various homes or states, even countries, during your life. Or you may have experienced only one or two places. Perhaps circumstances didn't allow for change. Maybe deep roots in one location have been positive for you or conversely, you felt like you were "doing time" in a particular place.

Places I have lived:

_____

_____

_____

_____

_____

_____

_____

_____

_____

_____

Power Places

If you're John Muir you want trees to
live among, If you're Emily, a garden
will do.
Try to find the right place for yourself.
If you can't find it, at least dream of it.[1]

These are the places that call me:

_____

_____

_____

_____

_____

_____

Why do I love these places? How do they reflect my spirit, and how do they support
and nourish me?

_____

_____

_____

_____

_____

_____

_____

_____

_____

_____

_____

1. Mary Oliver, "Leaves and Blossoms Along the Way," _Felicity: Poems_, Penguin, 2017.

When I cannot get to my power places, can I think of ways I might be able to recreate enough of what I experience there to restore my balance and inner peace?

_____

_____

_____

_____

_____

There are physical places in which we feel life more in flow, and there are physical places where we have greater difficulty connecting. Still, even those spaces we find difficult may assist us in identifying our values. An example of this might be having lived in a particularly unjust area that inspired sensitivity to many forms of injustice, leading us to a life of activism. Or perhaps living in a depressed, crime-ridden environment inspires us toward a life of creating peace, beauty, harmony, and mutual respect wherever we go. Maybe your unique self was positively impacting the place, simply by being there.

Where have I lived and not felt at home? Why was this the case?

You may also discover that no matter how much you try to have a role in a particular community, you simply cannot fully integrate and find your place. Still, that experience can be meaningful.

_____

_____

_____

_____

_____

_____

_____

What did I learn about myself and what is important to me as a result of living there?

_____

_____

_____

_____

_____

_____

What degree of social contact/solitude has been important to me? Do I find myself more energized by people or by alone time? What places have supported my needs and temperament? How have they done so?

_____

_____

_____

_____

_____

_____

Home as a Presence

Consider place and space in your current home. Later, you might also try this exercise with memories of the home where you grew up.

Do I feel like my home supports me as well as reflects my interests and tastes?

_____

_____

_____

_____

If a stranger were to walk into my home, what would they know about me by observing my space?

_____

_____

_____

_____

_____

_____

_____

David Spangler (teacher of "Incarnational Spirituality," and former codirector of Findhorn in Scotland) and his colleagues teach about the significance of our relationship with our living spaces. They suggest the exercise of energetically "feeling into" the different rooms in our homes as well as the land on which it rests.

Hallways and thresholds are the liminal spaces between different rooms and the states of consciousness we experience in them. For example, the function and feeling of a living room is very different from the bedroom, the bathroom, and the kitchen. Who we are in those spaces, the parts of ourselves we bring forward, and the activities they represent, differ significantly in quality. Giving attention to how we experience each room is an interesting exercise, heightening our appreciation of the space and sharpening our presence in them, while exercising our ability to consciously connect with what surrounds us.

After quietly spending some time with this exercise, aligning yourself with the energy of each room as well as the threshold spaces, consider your relationship with each room in your home. Take in the physical details of the space, the furniture, the decorations, the colors, etc.

How does each room feel to me? What part of me does each room support and activate? Where in the room am I typically most comfortable?

_____

_____

_____

_____

_____

_____

_____

_____

_____

_____

What about the closets, basement or attic, drawers, etc., the more hidden spaces? What do they feel like?

_____

_____

_____

_____

_____

If I were to encounter these rooms, including these hidden spaces in a dream, what information would they convey to me from my psyche? What might I need to attend to in my inner space?

_____

_____

_____

_____

_____

A pleasing choice of colors, placement of furniture, the right lighting, cleanliness, a sense of order and harmony, house plants, even appreciation for the room itself, all contribute to a sense of harmony or disharmony. Rituals such as burning incense or spraying the room with herb-infused or plain water, with the intent of clearing and cleaning the energetic space, can dramatically change the atmosphere in a room. Do the bones of the space—the walls, floors, ceilings, etc.—feel content? Is the space harmonious or not? If not, what could I do to bring a greater sense of harmony between me and the space?

_____

_____

_____

_____

_____

_____

_____

Land and its influence is similarly important to consider. In most indigenous and ancient cultures, the "spirits of the land" were considered living forces. These forces included the energy of the land itself and earth currents, as well as the spirits and subtle impressions of ancestors who lived there in the past.

Do I know the history of the land on which I dwell? Who was there before? Was there violence perpetrated on the land or on the people? How does the land *feel* to me now?

_____

_____

_____

_____

_____

_____

Physical care and simple appreciation contributes to the land. We are not just actors traveling through our lives with a backdrop of nature. Like the fish in the sea, we are a part of the land. Acknowledging its history is a powerful act of respect and gratitude.

How can I show gratitude to the land?

_____

_____

_____

_____

Our Relationship to the Natural World

The natural world, including animals, birds, fish, insects, and plants, can teach us so much. If you have had an animal-friend, then you know that it is a relationship of reciprocity. This reciprocal relationship is just as true if you have been a serious gardener or farmer. You have had a relationship with the world of plants and the earth herself. Beekeepers, too, experience a certain relationship with the bees and connection with their hives.

Our experiences with our animals are often ones of healing and growth through caring and responsibility. Our animal friends often soothe our hearts when nothing and no one else can. For many, animals are the only safe beings to love.

Animals in Our Lives

Hypnotherapist Robert Schwartz has encountered what his clients have described as "soul contracts" with their pets. These contracts have the goal of growth and support for both parties. It is a romantic idea, unprovable, but it can be used as a way into meaning, purpose, and appreciation.

Our animals each have a unique personality and can teach us by their example. They can demonstrate the virtues of unconditional love, presence, joy, independence, patience, courage, loyalty, and trust to their human caregivers. They can also be willful and stubborn. We can learn patience working with this too. They offer us real lessons and healing to the human heart hobbled by the carelessness and even cruelty of other humans.

It is interesting to note that because their life span is shorter than the typical human, they tend to pass on when we, ourselves, are about to make significant life changes. I have seen this time and again in the lives of clients and friends, as well as in my own experience. Perhaps their souls know they have done what they have come to do and that it's the right time for them to move on, giving us the freedom to make those changes.

With these thoughts in mind, let's take an additional deep dive into our relationships with animals and nature through the years.

If you have had animals in your life, list them here:

_____

_____

_____

_____

_____

_____

_____

_____

What are my strongest memories of the animals who have been in my life? Did we have an emotional connection? If so, what was this connection for me? Who do I remember most and why?

_____

_____

_____

_____

_____

_____

_____

_____

_____

_____

What traits most impressed me in each of them?

List the qualities that you most noted about their personalities and their characters.

_____

_____

_____

_____

_____

_____

_____

Were they teachers for me? Were they healers?

_____

_____

_____

_____

_____

_____

Did I grieve their loss, or did I put it aside? How and why? Do I have any regrets about how I processed or didn't process their loss?

_____

_____

_____

_____

_____

_____

_____

Do I ever feel an ongoing connection with them though they have passed?

There are many reports of pets appearing in dreams or synchronistic reminders many years after their passing.

_____

_____

_____

_____

_____

In what ways was I able to positively affect the life of my animal companions?

_____

_____

_____

_____

_____

Do I have any regrets about the way they were treated, or sadness if I failed to protect them? If so, can I tell them this message now as I write?

_____

_____

_____

_____

_____

_____

How might I honor their selfless service and companionship?

Honoring the animals that have passed in your life can be as simple as saying a heartfelt thank you, writing your pet a letter, setting up a photo within view, lighting a candle to remember them, or donating to an animal shelter or conservancy. Even a simple acknowledgement is valuable.

_____

_____

_____

_____

_____

_____

Can you imagine a response from your animal friend in return, here and now? Perhaps a feeling, a word, or an image may arise in your mind's eye. Allow yourself to trust this imagined response and say/feel a thank you in return.

What does my animal friend want to tell me?

_____

_____

_____

_____

_____

_____

The World of Plants

If I have devoted time to a garden or farming, what has that practice brought forward in me and/or taught me?

_____

_____

_____

_____

_____

_____

_____

Tending to a garden or even houseplants forms a relationship just like any other. What is my relationship to the plants in my care? How do they respond, or not, to me? What do I imagine they would like from me, and is that something I can do at this time?

_____

_____

_____

_____

_____

Memories

What are the most significant events during my thirties to fifties?

_____

_____

_____

_____

_____

_____

_____

What are my happiest memories during my thirties to fifties? What made them happy?

_____

_____

_____

_____

_____

How have these moments influenced my life moving forward?

_____

_____

_____

_____

_____

_____

_____

What are my most difficult memories during this period of my life?

_____

_____

_____

_____

_____

_____

_____

How have these memories influenced my life moving forward?

_____

_____

_____

_____

_____

_____

Working with Regret, An Honest View of Life

I used to feel proud to say that I regretted nothing in life until I read David Whyte. While I still believe that the unpleasant and sometimes tragic turns we take in life are part of our learning and never failures, I do appreciate David's honesty and his courage to own regrets. His perspective gave me the courage to consider my own regrets over some paths taken and some missed. Regrets are not an admission of weakness. They are simple reflections of our humanity.

Poet David Whyte writes this about regret:

> REGRET is a short, evocative and achingly beautiful word; an elegy to lost possibilities, even in its brief annunciation, it is also a rarity and almost never heard except where the speaker insists that they have none, that they are brave and forward-looking and could not possibly imagine their life in any other way than the way it is. To admit regret is to understand we are fallible, that there are powers in the world beyond *us*; to admit regret is to lose control not only of a difficult past but of the very story we tell about our present...The rarity of honest regret may be due to our contemporary emphasis on the youthful perspective...it takes a hard-won maturity to experience the depths of regret in ways that do not overwhelm and debilitate us but put us into a proper, more generous relationship with the future.

In his three-part workshop on shame, Whyte suggests a beautiful exercise of recalling a life episode in which you have experienced regret, then sitting quietly and scanning your body for what you feel. Identifying the feeling in our bodies expands our inner capacity to hold all our experience without needing to protect ourselves from what comes up. The capacity to hold regret and grief expands our maturity and availability to live life in the present because it brings down the walls we've erected against life and the soul.

Take a moment to consider an instance in your life that you regret. Listen to your body. What do you feel?

_____

_____

_____

_____

_____

_____

_____

_____

Have I been able to find opportunities for my own learning and growth even in the difficult memories?

Coming to peace with these events can take a lifetime or may not even be possible. But the question is offered here for contemplation and possibility.

_____

_____

_____

_____

_____

_____

_____

_____

How have these regrets influenced my life moving forward?

_____

_____

_____

_____

_____

_____

Please remember to use your personal journal if you feel the need to go deeper with processing.

Checking In

The Body

Consider the general feeling, tone, and experience you've had of your body during these years. Some examples might include experiencing your body as strong/vibrant, reliable, attractive, awkward/ugly, weak/insufficient, damaged, or as an obstacle. There will likely be a combination of experiences.

_____

_____

_____

_____

Do I experience my body as a friend and a reliable voice of what is and isn't in my best interest, physically and emotionally? Or have I mostly struggled in my relationship with my body?

In an era of harsh beauty standards, processed food that offers little real nourishment, and a sedentary and demanding lifestyle in the work world, many struggle with maintaining healthy weight and muscle, and even any conscious connection with the body except as a tool that works or looks or doesn't work or look the way we want it to.

_____

_____

_____

_____

_____

If my body had a voice, what would it like to tell me?

We have been having to relearn what was once natural to humans: listening to our bodies.

_____

_____

_____

_____

_____

Psyche and Soma (The Soul and the Body)

If we feel our bodies excessively demand unhealthy food or drink, consider what those cravings might signify on an emotional level. For example, a sugar tooth may be a literal expression of a craving for sweetness in life. An excessive desire for alcohol or cigarettes could be expressing a need for escape, comfort, comradery, transcendence of a difficult environment, or even a search for spirit.

Both alcohol and tobacco (in native tradition) have been used in sacred rituals. In a letter to Bill W., the founder of AA, dated January 30, 1961, Jung wrote this of a person they both knew: "(His) craving for alcohol was the equivalent, on a low level, of the spiritual thirst of our being for wholeness, expressed in medieval language: the union with God." In seeking escape from a sense of deep alienation and disconnection from spirit, we may turn to spirits.

Consider what any excessive food and drink cravings or dependencies might be signifying emotionally.

What is my psyche calling for through these cravings?

_____

_____

_____

_____

_____

What might I start doing to address these deeper needs?

_____

_____

_____

_____

_____

_____

The Heart

What has been my experience on a heart level during this period of my life?

Some examples might include open/joyful, fearful/careful, confused, or broken/sad/helpless. Use these or your own descriptions.

_____

_____

_____

_____

_____

_____

If my heart had a voice, what would it want to tell me? What does it need?

_____

_____

_____

_____

_____

_____

The Mind

How about my mind? What has been the general tenor of my thoughts between the ages of thirty to fifty? Examples might include excited, stimulated, creative, depressed, stressed, etc.

_____

_____

_____

_____

_____

If you are experiencing ongoing depression or anxiety, please consult your physician. There could be a biological cause. Medication can be helpful in managing symptoms while you work on addressing the cause with a trained and experienced counselor or therapist. In addition, healthy changes in nutrition, sleep routines, and exercise, as well as being in nature offer simple but powerful assistance in establishing a healthy mental state.

The Spirit

And on a spiritual level, what have I experienced in my 30's-50's? Examples might include a sense of connection/joy, alienation, numbness, etc.

_____

_____

_____

_____

_____

What could I do to feel more joy and connection in my life moving forward?

_____

_____

_____

_____

_____

_____

_____

What would my Soul say, if I invited it to speak?

_____

_____

_____

_____

_____

_____

Concerns and Challenges

What have been my biggest concerns and challenges during these years?

_____

_____

_____

_____

_____

Am I satisfied with how I have managed them? Do I feel I have grown?
In what ways?

_____

_____

_____

_____

_____

_____

_____

_____

_____

Themes and Patterns

What have been the major themes in my adult life?

_____

_____

_____

_____

_____

_____

What patterns do I notice repeating through these years, and possibly recurring since adolescence and childhood?

_____

_____

_____

_____

_____

_____

Has there been an evolution in how I navigate these patterns? How am I evolving?

_____

_____

_____

_____

_____

What do I need to thrive and be at my best?

_____
_____
_____
_____
_____
_____

What inhibits, represses, and diminishes my joy and self-expression?

_____
_____
_____
_____
_____
_____

What sustains me?

_____
_____
_____
_____
_____
_____

My Alchemical Journey: Part Three

The story continues. The spiral of time has moved forward through the years. Continue where you left off at the end of your adolescent years. Your adventures and encounters have involved both love and work. All seeming failures can be seen as opportunities to learn and grow. Whether fated or chosen, they offer opportunities for our evolution. They are the ingredients of our life's alchemical project.

To Review

The Four Alchemical Phases are The Nigredo (a burning away of the old), the Albedo (a respite in which there is the beginning of a new expression), the Citrinitas (in which you are actively preparing for a new life and self-expression), and the Rubedo (a fulfillment, you step into a new, more relevant and truer identity).

Remember that psychologically and spiritually we travel the phases and stages in a circular fashion as we make the conscious journey through life, growing and changing.

The Seven Substages include:

Calcinatio – the burning away of your old identity. It is a difficult, highly uncomfortable process symbolized by fire.

Dissolutio – a dissolution. A washing away of "the ashes of what once was," to make way for the new. It is too early to make sense of things. The best approach is to allow the "unknowing," while trusting the process. This phase includes water imagery.

Separatio – beginning to make sense of what has occurred. You make new choices that often require a cutting away of situations and relationships that no longer resonate with who you are becoming. This is the "airy," mental phase.

Coniunctio – a new sense of wholeness, but on a more refined level. Your heart and your mind are more in sync. Your values have become clearer and your choices more reflective of your authentic self. There is a sense of peace psychologically.

This phase is represented by weddings and sexual union imagery.

Fermentatio – a further purification. Remaining aspects of the psyche that obscure your true "light," undergo a rotting phase, and Spirit or your Higher Self get involved in the transmutation. All rotting images apply.

Distillatio – you are undergoing even more refinement as a soul, free of ego inflation. Dream images often include flying, climbing to the top of a mountain, and meeting lions or eagles. Meditation, contemplation, prayer, and all mystical endeavors assist the Work. You have greater access to the clarity of discernment regarding yourself, your relationships, and the state of the world.

Coagulatio – more than the marriage of opposites experienced in the coniunctio, you achieve a new fusion. In *Coagulatio*, the opposites are entirely integrated in our psyche. The androgyne (the perfect blend of male and female) is symbolic of this achievement. The heart and the mind, matter and spirit, are united. A new, authentic confidence is achieved and a sense of wholeness that is unshakeable. Clarity of mind and compassion of the heart are fully awakened and present.

Having achieved *Coagulatio*, you are more authentically complete, with a solid sense of confidence in who you are. But this does not mean you will not experience some aspects of the earlier stages from time to time. Life is not stagnant but ever in process.

On the lines below, consider the alchemical processes as they have shown up during these years:

What were the major events in your life during your thirties and forties? What were your most pressing concerns in each decade? What burned away, what was dissolved? How did your thoughts and values shift? Who were you becoming? What was evolving in you and how did that impact your life? What progress did you make?

What am I working on? Where am I with themes such as self-care, self-worth, confidence, empathy, compassion, respect, discernment, boundaries, personal sovereignty, and any values I have wanted to develop?

_____

_____

_____

_____

Photo Memories

Part Three and a Half

Middlescence

What is Middlescence?

"Middlescence" is the season of our lives when we transition from adulthood to elderhood. Coined by the founder of the Modern Elder Academy, Chip Conley, the term echoes "adolescence," the years of biological and psychological transition from childhood to adulthood.

The wheel of life turns once again when we reach middlescence. Our lives are cyclic, not linear. If we have evolved through the years, we won't just repeat the cycle of our lives, we will have spiraled upward into the next stage of our unfolding.

Health as We Grow Older: Burning Away the Dross

Just as in adolescence, both women and men undergo changes in these middlescent years. Hormone levels shift, moving the body away from its focus on physical generativity, offering the potential for a more inward perspective and great personal creativity.

Changes in the Male Body

Men experience changes in their physical energy, health, and capabilities. Their sense of identity, value, and purpose shifts, especially as their needs in the workplace change and they face ageism. Men who have relied on a strong, capable body all their lives, often grieve the loss of strength and ability.

As a man, how do I view growing older? What is the downside? What could be the benefits?

_____

_____

_____

_____

_____

_____

_____

What changes am I experiencing in my body during this transition period?

_____

_____

_____

_____

Am I coming to terms with the reality of those changes? How am I handling them? Am I respectful of my body? How am I taking care of myself?

In a youth-driven culture, fear can propel drastic and physically traumatizing reactions to normal body changes. It's important to balance exercise and cosmetic services with respect for the body.

_____

_____

_____

_____

_____

_____

_____

_____

What are my greatest challenges at this time of life?

_____

_____

_____

_____

_____

Can I find any positives—mentally, emotionally, and spiritually—that were either not present or less so in my earlier years? Has age brought its own gifts?

In contemporary culture, men have mostly been valued for their ability to achieve in the world. As the body ages, much of that acumen suffers. What if the purpose of the coming years is *inner* achievement? What if now a man can focus on his own inner world, as well as feelings and relationship, freed from the insistence of hormones and more public success?

Every life season has its gifts, though at first glance, one may only notice loss. In the space below, begin to imagine what those gifts might be.

‗‗

‗‗

‗‗

‗‗

‗‗

‗‗

‗‗

‗‗

Changes in the Female Body

Just as girls experience menstruation for the first time in adolescence, women experience a visible and dramatic transition entering their perimenopause, menopause, and post-menopausal years. For a few women, this transition comes early in life, but for the majority it happens in their fifties. This transition can take anywhere from four to twelve or more years to complete. It begins with irregular menstrual periods and progressively more frequent hot flashes as the body readjusts hormonal levels.

Some women experience eruptions of rage and sadness, similar to earlier monthly mood fluctuations, and sometimes to a far more intense degree. It has been theorized that a patriarchal society that discourages females from expressing anger may have produced girls and women who have been taught overtly or subliminally to repress their natural feelings of anger. What has been suppressed will find a way to express itself.

Just as menstruation is a cleansing time, both physically for the womb as well as psychologically, menopause similarly produces hormonal changes. Hot flashes replace the cramping of her early periods, as the body makes way for a new orientation, physically, psychologically, and spiritually.

The mostly male medical establishment has pathologized menopause, encouraging hormone replacement to women as an effort to ward off this very natural transition. For some, this may be a needed relief. But for many, it is more of a compliance with the glorification of youth by our culture. Only very recently has menopause become a subject of discussion with a new appreciation for our natural bodily changes.

The centuries of the prevailing patriarchal view that women lose their value once their bodies lose their youthful standards of beauty and vigor and are no longer physically fertile is being challenged by many feminist writers. Just as we need to recover from the inculcated cultural shame of our monthly bleeding, it's valuable and healthy to honor and explore the gifts of moving on from our years of physical fertility. The coming years can be our most mentally, emotionally, and spiritually fertile and the most personally fulfilling.

For many women, post menopause is a time of incredible creativity. These years offer us a golden opportunity to step into an earned personal power and sovereignty. A woman is able, at last, to define herself not by who she is to others (daughter, wife, parent, etc.), but by who she is in herself. Jungian psychoanalyst and author, Nor Hall, describes this time in a woman's life as a return to a psychological "virginity":

> "The word virgin means 'belonging-to-no-man'...Virgin means one-in-herself; not maiden inviolate, but maiden alone, in-herself. To be virginal does not mean to be chaste, but rather to be true to nature and instinct."[1]

Nor Hall references both M. Esther Harding's work on women's mysteries and John Layard's essay, "The Incest Taboo and the Virgin Archetype," in the Virgin Archetype. She describes virginity as spiritual pregnancy. Monica Sjoo, too, in *The Great Cosmic Mother*, along with others, has written about a new/old definition of "virgin." Echoing Hall, they have interpreted the word to mean "she who is owned by no one, who is, in and of herself." This definition arises from the Greek word for virgin, "Parthenos," having more to do with autonomy than sex. It evokes a sense of internal identity and is not derived from physical events. During menopause, a woman reclaims her virginity, re-orienting her in a new direction, offering potential for great personal creativity.

1. Nor Hal, *The Moon and the Virgin*, New York, HarperPerennial, 1994., p.11.

In the Arthurian legend of "Gawain and the Lady Ragnelle," a riddle is posed to King Arthur. Only if it is solved correctly will his life be spared by the Black Knight. The question posed is this: "What does a woman desire most?" After receiving many false responses from women across the land, his nephew and trusted knight, Gawain, receives the correct answer from the Lady Ragnelle herself. The answer is "Women desire sovereignty." As we move toward elderhood, we rightfully claim our sovereignty, hard-won from experience.

Menopause, at whatever age, presents these considerations. You are no longer a conduit for physical life, but you are even more available to be a channel for the gifts of the mind and spirit. The potential of these gifts is no less worthy than the creation of a new human on this earth.

If I've gone through menopause, when did it begin and how did it affect me? If I have not yet reached menopause, how do I envision that transition—the losses and the gains?

_____

_____

_____

_____

_____

_____

While many women mourn the diminishment of their societally sanctioned sexual allure, there is also a physical freedom that comes as a result, particularly in a patriarchal world. Whereas many women relish the feeling of sexual desirability, it is often accompanied by subtle and not so subtle signs of danger. Women, at this stage, no longer feel the same degree of sexual threat that might have accompanied them before on any walk alone through the city or in nature.

What is my experience with this?

_____

_____

_____

_____

_____

_____

How can I best keep my body healthy at this age, while being respectful of the changes I'm undergoing?

In a youth-driven culture, fear can propel drastic and physically traumatizing reactions to normal body changes. It's important to balance exercise, diet, and cosmetic services with respect for the body.

_____

_____

_____

_____

_____

_____

Memories

What are my most beautiful, happy memories from this time?

_____

_____

_____

_____

_____

_____

How have these moments influenced my life moving forward?

_____

_____

_____

_____

_____

_____

_____

What have been my most difficult memories?

_____

_____

_____

_____

_____

Have I been able to find any opportunity for learning and growth?

_____

_____

_____

_____

_____

_____

_____

How have memories of the past influenced me during this period in my life?

_____

_____

_____

_____

_____

How to Update your Desires

How can I update my desires of the past?

What could I do now that might achieve the feelings I still want to experience?

_____

_____

_____

_____

_____

_____

_____

_____

_____

_____

_____

_____

_____

_____

_____

_____

_____

_____

_____

_____

Checking In

The Body

How do I experience my body?

_____

_____

_____

_____

If my body had a voice, what would it want to tell me?

If you've had any challenges with a part of your body, it can be extremely useful to create a written dialogue with it. Ask your body questions. Answers may arrive that surprise and enlighten you.

_____

_____

_____

_____

_____

_____

_____

What do I want to say to my body?

_____

_____

_____

_____

_____

This conversation can start an ongoing dialogue, both about your own attitude toward your body and its messages for you.

The Heart

What is my experience of this time on a feeling level? How is my emotional and physical heart? Do I experience any sensations in my heart area? What are they?

Some examples might include open/joyful, fearful/vigilant, confused, broken/sad/helpless. Use these or your own descriptions.

_____

_____

_____

_____

_____

_____

If my heart had a voice, what would it want to tell me?

_____

_____

_____

_____

_____

_____

What would I tell my heart?

_____

_____

_____

_____

_____

_____

The Mind

How about my mind during this life transition? What is the general tenor of my thoughts?

Examples might include excited, stimulated/creative, grateful, joyful, peaceful, depressed, anxious, hopeless, helpless, rumination, etc. There may be a combination of thoughts.

_____

_____

_____

_____

_____

Maybe you are experiencing some differences in memory and processing. If so, how are you feeling about and managing these changes? What are you doing to keep in the best mental shape? Where are you with acceptance?

_____

_____

_____

_____

_____

Some Thoughts about Depression and Anxiety

Every significant life transition can unsettle us. If you are having trouble navigating this or any of the life stages, you may be suffering from depression or anxiety, Depression is frequently triggered by a feeling of loss and powerlessness. Anxiety is triggered by a hypervigilance rooted in fearful anticipation of the future. Any prolonged suffering of mind is the psyche's call for help. It is important to relay any symptoms to your doctor. There could be a biological imbalance.

Hormonal changes, chemical shifts, and genes can trigger depression and anxiety just as much as psychological causes.

Depression can be a normal response to loss, as in the case of a death of someone close to us, the ending of a close relationship, or a catastrophic world event. Ask for help. Grief groups, for example, are of great assistance in processing a loss of a loved one whether through death or divorce. This is also a good time to consider psychotherapy. Enlisting a trained and empathic counselor for assistance in navigating debilitating grief, fear, anger or apathy, can lead to release of stuck feeling, a healthy shift in our thoughts, integration of old wounds, and a renewed experience of freedom and pleasure.

There are also times when we might experience what has been called a "creative depression," a time of incubation, in which we feel a lack of motivation. We experience a quiescence, a quiet inward turning, in preparation for a creative renaissance. It is important to consider what sort of depression we are experiencing. No one explanation or solution fits all cases.

Anxiety stems from a focus on the past or the future. Focusing on the present (mindfulness practices teach us this) stills the anxious mind. Anxiety can also be managed by slowing down and deepening the breath, a resource that is available to all of us at no cost. It is such a simple technique that people often overlook its fantastic power to calm the mind and the body. Calming our physiology, slow deep breaths bring us back into balance. You cannot go into panic if you are breathing slowly and evenly.

Another useful strategy is the progressive relaxation of the muscles in the body, from the feet up or the face and neck down. It is a simple technique of progressively squeezing and then releasing the muscles in the face and body. It is also a great method to use when you have a hard time falling asleep. Additionally, a simple To Do list before bed can help the mind to let go and set worries aside for the night. A final suggestion is the EFT method (the Emotional Freedom Techniques) of tapping various parts of the body in a prescribed sequence. The tapping progressively reduces the energy in our anxious thoughts until the experience becomes neutral. EFT instruction is readily available online.

Both depression and anxiety are relieved by calming our neurological system. Body work, including traditional massage and the more specialized somatic therapy, are a few ways to address a heightened sense of anxiety, while therapeutic touch can help relieve feelings of alienation and disconnection that so often accompany depression.

The best combination of help involves addressing your thoughts, feelings, and sometimes your history with an experienced counselor; restructuring your diet to be more nutritious; getting better sleep; and, when needed, getting the assistance of medication to regulate the body's chemistry. Making time to be in nature is both balancing and healing.

Limiting intake of negative media is good practice too, especially of fear-based news or even fictional stories that increase the adrenalin. Instead, we might seek out and align ourselves with causes that help heal these wide-spread problems, and in so doing, get the added benefit of connecting with supportive others. This can make a real difference in us and for our communities.

We are living in a world of extremes and massive change. It's both a time of great light and chaotic darkness. The news we hear most often reports the darkness, encouraging feelings helplessness and fear. It is hardly pathological that we might feel anxiety and depression. We can be activists in the world, doing our part to make a better world with big or small day-to-day actions, and acting as activists behind the scenes when we cultivate our joy and faith in a better, more sane future. It is vitally important that we learn good self-care and find a way to hold our light through these times.

If my thoughts are consistently troubled, what resources can I find to create a more peaceful and healthful state of mind?

_____

_____

_____

_____

_____

_____

_____

Are there any like-minded communities available to me?

If this is resonant, what can you do to get involved? They could be communities involved in activism creating social change, politics, or meditation etc. Not everyone is an activist out in the world. Some are activists through good works and even as meditators for peace. Go with your interests or try something new. Consider where you feel a call.

_____

_____

_____

_____

The Spirit

On a spiritual level, what do or did I experience in my *"middlescence?"*

Examples might include a sense of connection, joy, alienation, numbness, etc. Again, consider the complexity of your own experience.

_____

_____

_____

_____

_____

_____

What does my soul (my deeper self) want to tell me about this time in my life?

_____

_____

_____

_____

_____

_____

How do I hope to feel as I move forward in or from this era of my life?

_____

_____

_____

_____

_____

_____

In what areas do I feel I have grown psychologically as well as spiritually? Where do I feel I am in my personal alchemical work and why?

_____

_____

_____

_____

_____

_____

My Alchemical Journey: Part 3 1/2

Review the Alchemical phases as outlined in My Alchemical Journey: Part 3. What has been your alchemical process in your fifties? Which substages most apply? What overall phase or phases feel resonant to these years?

_____

_____

_____

_____

_____

_____

_____

_____

_____

_____

_____

_____

_____

_____

_____

_____

_____

_____

_____

_____

_____

Part Four

Elderhood –
The Wisdom
Years

Elderhood can be divided into three distinct stages: The Young Elder (typically sixty to seventy years), The Seasoned Elder (seventy to eighty years), and the The PhD, or Sovereign Elder (eighty and beyond). All three stages offer an invitation to further develop the Sage and the Wise Woman. In our elder years, it is our task to own our worth and share our gifts with those who will follow us.

In contrast to the term "elderly," which connotes infirmity, Elder is an honorific title, awarded for lifetime experience and achievement. Indigenous tribes worldwide honor their Elders as bearers of broad experience and deep wisdom. They not only hold a place of honor in the community but are consulted by the younger members on both personal and public matters.

To reach elderhood, one has traveled the long road, hopefully having grown in the values of patience and the long view. Clearly, not every old person is an Elder, but we live in a culture that overvalues youth and dismisses the old, while extending the human lifespan through advances in medicine. A model that respects a growing mature population is sorely needed. The days of drearily warehousing our old people until they die must come to an end. It is time to remember how to promote a culture that respects its elders and finds ways in which they can contribute to the greater community. Rather than focusing on decline, a healthy culture supports, honors, and finds appropriate contributions for the mental, emotional, and spiritual maturity of its elders.

This recultivation of a healthier awareness of aging in Western contemporary culture is necessary. A positive sign of this revolution are some new ways of caring for our elders, one example being elder communes and cooperative living situations, in which there is both privacy and shared space for occupants, as well as the opportunity to maintain some personal autonomy and dignity while getting access to needed nutritional and health care.

What is positive Eldering?

Clearly it is not about pontificating to the young or over-sentimentalizing the past. Nor is it telling the same stories time and again without any positive message or lessons learned. Ruminating usually occurs alongside disappointment, feeling like life no longer holds value. Often rumination is the result of unprocessed trauma.

In contrast, the goal of elderhood is to move into the Sage/Wise Woman who has mastered the compassionate view that everyone is allowed their own path, while accepting that path will surely include detours. Elders are aware of the cyclic nature and the pendulum swing of history. They don't get carried away by fads and fanaticism. They honor the forward momentum leading to the future, with a wise eye to the past. They also know what is of lasting importance: our relationships to the earth and to each other. The best eldering displays compassion alongside the knowledge—the formula for true wisdom, won from a life well lived and considered.

If we value consciousness, this is the era in which life review becomes our primary task. What follows are some questions to help you put all those life pieces together.

Reviewing the Past

When did it happen?
"It was a long time ago."

Where did it happen?
"It was far away."

No, tell. Where did it happen?
"In my heart."

What is your heart doing now?
"Remembering, Remembering!"[1]

How have you grown, and in what ways, since childhood/young adulthood?
How have you blossomed? You have been invited to contemplate this question
throughout this workbook. Here are some questions to get to the heart of it.

What fears do I recall having as a child and young adult? Which ones have I
overcome?

_____

_____

_____

_____

_____

_____

_____

_____

_____

1. Mary Oliver, "When Did It Happen?" *Felicity,* Penguin Books, 2017.

What major challenges have I met? What have been my successes?

Include successes in your relationships as well as in your work or profession.

_____
_____
_____
_____
_____
_____
_____
_____
_____

How are my choices different from what I would have chosen at earlier stages in life? How have I shifted and evolved?

Your *answer can include choice of friends, partners, environment, entertainment, diet, and interests.*

_____
_____
_____
_____
_____
_____
_____
_____
_____

What are some of the things I have learned about life, having lived this many years?

_____

_____

_____

_____

_____

_____

_____

_____

_____

What do I know now about myself, the person I am? Who have I grown into?

_____

_____

_____

_____

_____

_____

_____

How am I the same? What feels intrinsic to my unique signature in life?

We all can recognize the I that we are no matter the passage of time. There is a core that remains through childhood, adolescence and the different stages of adulthood. We can explore who we are by what has called to us consistently throughout our lives, in one form or another.

During childhood and adolescence, maybe you loved books, or liked to entertain others by performing. Maybe you were a natural leader. Maybe you pretended that you were a nurse or a mother of an imaginary family. Maybe you pretended to be a teacher or a warrior. Maybe science fascinated you. Did you love to build things or take things apart and put them back together? Perhaps you played at several of these roles. These are just a few examples.

Though they evolved into new expressions, often the seeds of your life's signature and mission were visible even then.

_____

_____

_____

_____

_____

_____

_____

_____

Do I feel like any parts of me still lie dormant, somehow squelched or frozen through choice or life circumstances? Are there any talents and interests I would still like to explore and develop?

These years often provide us with a new freedom to explore.

_____

_____

_____

_____

_____

_____

_____

_____

294 Elderhood / THE ALCHEMY OF YOUR LIFE

Do circumstances allow for me to pursue this interest/talent now, or is it best to come to acceptance of what is?

For example, if you wanted to master another language, is it time to seriously pursue fluency or do you need to amend that goal? You could decide advanced fluency isn't practical, but you can still enjoy and benefit from conversation classes or even just visit that country and appreciate what you already know. You can apply this to any skill you have been hoping to master but hadn't the time and opportunity earlier in life.

_____

_____

_____

_____

_____

_____

Redefining and Curating Your Elderhood

What do I believe about aging?

Often, we absorb beliefs from the surrounding culture, including what the media portrays. Maybe the versions of age we experienced as we were growing up reflected debilitation and a failure to move with the times. What has been your picture of aging in the past? Have you questioned these views as you've gotten older? Do these beliefs have to be true for you?

_____

_____

_____

_____

_____

_____

_____

Describe a life affirming, positive vision of the Elderhood. What are its benefits? What can be its joys and satisfactions?

_____

_____

_____

_____

_____

_____

_____

Stepping into our Authority

The Tarot Court Cards offer archetypal metaphors for our maturation. Younger persons are assigned Page, Princess, and Knight, while the Queen and King express achievement and maturity. Admittedly, there are far more possibilities available today than those gleaned from the feudal system. Certainly, girls today identify with more than Princess. Nevertheless, these archetypes perennially serve as shorthand for our evolution.

In essence, they point to the potential of stepping into our personal authority as we age. To grow into a Queen or King is to achieve personal "sovereignty." This has nothing to do with domination of others. "Sovereignty" is used here in the same way we saw "virgin" expressed earlier designating a woman as "One unto Herself," owned by no one, i.e., Whole. Likewise, "Kings" and "Queens" demonstrate a tempered maturity and Wholeness. The four elemental suits (fire, water, air and earth) of the Tarot, describe differing temperaments and focus, but the evolution toward a mature expression is the same.

Maintaining access to the gifts of earlier stages enhances our experience and our range. We may evolve into a Queen or King, but we benefit from being able to play like the Page and Princess, and adventure like the Knight, experiencing the romance of life.

It must be remembered that no one is purely feminine or masculine. We contain both, no matter which body we received at birth, or that we choose. Our expression runs the spectrum between the two poles, often depending upon our relationships. For example, we tend to step into what is needed by our circumstances, and we often spontaneously express the complement of our partners or coworkers. Our life circumstances calls us to lean into one side or the other.

As we grow older, we may find ourselves living into a formerly unlived side of ourselves. A very feminine woman who focused on mothering in her youth may find she starts to develop an interest in achievement outside of this role. Conversely, men who have focused on career achievement may begin to place greater emphasis on the value of relationship and nurturing others. As our culture becomes more fluid, these shifts appear to have emerged earlier and more visibly at any life stage.

Whether we identify as a man or a woman, trans or non-binary, we all carry a yin/yang to varying degrees and neither side of ourselves is superior to the other. Each is needed for human wholeness.

Do I still have access to the wonder of childhood and the enthusiasm of youth?

The wonder of childhood is represented by the Page in the tarot court cards, while the enthusiasm of youth is depicted as the Knight. Hopefully, we have preserved the creative liveliness of spirit from younger versions of ourselves, adding a felt sense of fulfillment and a more satisfying and whole sense of self to our elder years.

Is the youthful curiosity, innocence and purity of the Page still available to me? How so?

_____

_____

_____

_____

Do I still feel the adventurous energy of the Knight? How so?

_____

_____

_____

_____

Have I developed the inner Queen and/or King? Do I feel that I stand in my own *sovereignty*, far less thrown off balance by circumstances, situations, and other people's opinions or drama?

_____

_____

_____

_____

Do I honor my long experience? Do I feel it has deepened into wisdom? If not, can I make this a goal?

Wisdom is achieved through the marriage of knowledge (born of experience) and compassion.

_____

_____

_____

_____

_____

Curate the vision of yourself as an honored and honorable Elder. What do you want to embody?

Who do you want to be in your full flowering of this life?

Consider archetypes that inspire you. For example: the Matriarch/Patriarch, the Guardian of the Tribe, or the Wild Elder (someone who is deeply connected with nature). There are many more archetypes available. Look up more or create one that best describes your vision for yourself at this stage. Elderhood can be seen as your achievement, the well-earned crown after many of life's challenges.

Who do I want to be as an Elder? What qualities do I want to define me?

_____

_____

_____

_____

_____

_____

_____

How do I contribute to life at this stage of my journey? Are there any other ways that call to me?

A simple voiced appreciation of others, offering a smile to a stranger, creating a comfortable home for family and friends, listening patiently and compassionately to others, helping with grandchildren, caring for animals and nature, political and environmental service and activism are all ways to contribute. No positive act is inconsequential.

_____

_____

_____

_____

_____

_____

_____

_____

Relationships

If I am in a partnership, how do I currently view my relationship? What do I value in it?

_____

_____

_____

_____

_____

_____

What are the best parts of my relationship with my partner? What can I do to sustain and expand the best of Us?

_____

_____

_____

_____

_____

As no one person can fulfill all my needs, with who else in my life—friends and extended community—can I pursue the interests that my partner doesn't share?

_____

_____

_____

How is my relationship with my partner changing? Do I have any fears regarding my relationship?

_____

_____

_____

_____

_____

_____

Self-care is essential if you are in a caregiving role!

If you are in the position of caring for an ailing partner, do you have help? If not, can you think of resources to assist you? Make a list below of ways you can find support. This list could include family members, friends, and community services. You will need breaks to restore yourself, mentally, emotionally, and physically.

If you are caring for a terminally ill person, hospice organizations can provide contact information for places that offer "respite care," freeing up caregivers for a week or two to restore themselves.

_____

_____

_____

_____

How have I grown through the years of partnership?

_____

_____

_____

_____

_____

_____

_____

If I am single, what value do I find in my independence?

_____

_____

_____

_____

_____

_____

What about the downsides of being single? How do I compensate for them?

_____

_____

_____

_____

What is my relationship to sexuality and sensuality, especially touch? What do I need? How do or can I get these needs met?

_____

_____

_____

_____

_____

_____

_____

_____

Adult Children

What are my relationships with each of my grown children?

_____
_____
_____
_____
_____
_____
_____

How about my relationships with their partners?

_____
_____
_____
_____
_____
_____
_____
_____

What are my hopes for these relationships? How do I want them to be? If I would like them to improve, what can I do on my end?

_____
_____
_____
_____

_____

_____

_____

_____

If You Have Grandchildren and Great-Grandchildren

How is our relationship? How do I hope it to be?

_____

_____

_____

_____

_____

If any of these relationships are less than wished for, is there anything I can do to bring us closer?

_____

_____

_____

_____

What are my hopes for my grandchildren? What can I do to actualize these hopes?

_____

_____

_____

_____

_____

_____

_____

_____

Do I have any concerns about any of my family relationships?

_____

_____

_____

_____

_____

_____

_____

What can I do to mitigate those concerns?

_____

_____

_____

_____

_____

_____

If I am unable to effect a change in my family's dynamics, can I come to acceptance?

Our adult children have their own lives and "karma." They are adults now and no longer children. If our help or intervention is unwelcome, we need to let them work things out for themselves in their own time. Maybe we can view this opening as an opportunity to focus our attention elsewhere toward the places in life that bring us joy and satisfaction.

_____

_____

_____

_____

_____

Friendships

Which relationships are most important to me now and why?

_____

_____

_____

_____

_____

How do I cultivate and tend our connection? Is there more that I can do if I feel our relationships aren't what they could be?

_____

_____

_____

_____

_____

Community

Traditional cultures always include their elders in the community. The isolation and alienation so many elders experience today is a cultural pathology. It benefits neither the individual nor the larger community. Elders who have satisfying community and personal relationships have more life force and joy, experiencing a real sense of contribution and connection.

If I am feeling isolated, can I think of ways to further connect and feel more of a valued and valuable part of the community?

_____

_____

_____

_____

_____

_____

Do I have connection with community? Who and what do I consider my communities?

_____

_____

_____

_____

_____

_____

Are they satisfying and why? If not, why not?

_____

_____

_____

_____

_____

_____

Are there any contributions I still hope to make to the world?

_____

_____

_____

_____

_____

How might I put these aspirations into action?

_____

_____

_____

_____

_____

What about my legacy? What do I hope to leave for my family and community?

This answer can include intangibles like a sense of pride, safety, etc., and/or a physical legacy of property, resources, and creative works.

_____

_____

_____

_____

_____

_____

How do I hope to be remembered by my family, friends, and community?

_____

_____

_____

_____

_____

_____

What actions can I take to make this a meaningful and joyful life chapter?

_____

_____

_____

_____

_____

_____

Letting Go

Storage

When I moved from one house to another
there were many things I had no room
for. What does one do? I rented a storage
space. And filled it. Years passed.
Occasionally I went there and looked in,
but nothing happened, not a single
twinge of the heart.
As I grew older the things I cared
about grew fewer, but were more
important. So one day I undid the lock
and called the trash man. He took
everything.
I felt like the little donkey when
his burden finally lifted. Things!
Burn them, burn them! Make a beautiful
fire! More room in your heart for love,
for the trees! For the birds who own
nothing—the reason they can fly.[1]

How do I feel about letting go of possessions in my life? What things are valuable to me now? Have I become more discriminating about what I own and what I can let go?

_____

_____

_____

_____

_____

_____

1. Mary Oliver, "Storage," *Felicity*, Penguin Books, 2017.

Loss of a life partner and friends is inevitable if we live long enough. Aging calls for a growing surrender. Gradually, or not so gradually, our physical strength lessens, and friends and maybe our life partner passes. All of this is nature's way of preparing us to let go and move on. Readying *our* hearts for these losses does not make them hurt less, but we can begin cultivating acceptance before the time comes.

Have I lost friends (through death)? Who? How am I feeling about these losses?

_____

_____

_____

_____

_____

_____

How am I managing these loses?

_____

_____

_____

_____

_____

_____

_____

If there is life after death, who do I imagine *I* will miss the most when I'm no longer here?

_____

_____

_____

_____

_____

_____

If these people are living, do they know how special they are to me? How might I convey their importance to me?

_____

_____

_____

_____

_____

_____

Old Betrayals and Abandonment

Do I have any regrets about broken relationships? What are those regrets?

_____

_____

_____

_____

_____

_____

May Your Heart Be Light as a Feather

The ancient Egyptians taught that our (emotional) hearts are weighed after death. One could not go on to the best afterlife unless one's heart "weighed less than a feather." When we carry the burden of bitterness and resentment, our hearts are heavy.

Forgiveness is key—not of the crimes against us, but of the *ignorance* of the people who hurt or disappointed us. Sometimes we also need to forgive *ourselves* for our own ignorance and less-than-ideal outcomes in our lives. We live in a world in which we all have less than perfect clarity. Much of what goes wrong is due to pain, ignorance, and fear, leading inevitably to selfishness, greed, and violence. Acknowledging our human condition, as we have inherited it, can serve to lighten the weight caused by betrayal, loss, and oppression.

Enduring resentment and regret may also represent a longing for a different and perfect story, one without pain and fear. We may wish for this but believing there is an ideal existence devoid of suffering denies the complexity of our human experience. Hanging onto resentment and regret, as an ongoing narrative, keeps up stuck in the past, creating a rigidity that denies life and the freedom to live fully in the present.

Until we address the stagnant, festering resentments and regrets, we carry them with us. We may not be able to entirely remove these marks on our hearts but facing them honestly and coming to terms with them will lighten the load, easing the path to let go of this life in peace. We will have done our part of the work.

Not all relationships can be addressed directly. Sometimes a person who has hurt us or whom we have hurt has died or moved away. Contact could or would not be appropriate. Still, we can make subtle contact with them through journaling, meaningful ritual and writing letters we never send. Perhaps, on a subliminal level, those letters are still received.

When my mother was dying, many memories of broken relationships from decades past resurfaced. While her body was in the process of shutting down, crystal clear memories of betrayals that had occurred over fifty years prior emerged from her unconscious. Perhaps her psyche was attempting to process this old material.

From my incomplete vantage point, accompanying her through her dying, she seemed unable to resolve and let these things go before she passed. On the other hand, my father-in-law, a holocaust survivor who had spent several years in Auschwitz, came to terms with his past a decade before his death, by attending survivor healing groups and volunteering to educate others about tolerance in his elderhood. He passed peacefully.

Are there any unfinished, broken relationships that I would like to conclude gracefully for my own peace of mind and of heart?

Name these relationships:

_____

_____

_____

_____

_____

_____

_____

_____

I still feel _____ (for example, grief, discomfort, anxiety, anger, etc.) about what happened with _____.

Name each person who comes to mind and describe what occurred.

_____

_____

_____

_____

_____

_____

_____

_____

Are there any events in my life that still weigh heavily on my heart?

_____

_____

_____

_____

_____

_____

_____

_____

_____

_____

If I still struggle with thoughts of loss and betrayal in the past, how might I address the pain and memory of these experiences to clear their toxicity? Is there a perspective that might help with this?

_____

_____

_____

_____

_____

_____

_____

_____

Can I make any meaning from these experiences, or at least find a purpose in them?

_____

_____

_____

_____

_____

_____

_____

_____

How did these events influence my life and, by extension, the lives of my loved ones as life unfolded?

_____

_____

_____

_____

_____

_____

_____

What did I learn about myself and about navigating the world from these experiences?

_____

_____

_____

_____

_____

_____

_____

Is there anything I would do differently, given a second chance? How have I grown since going through these moments of pain and betrayal?

_____

_____

_____

_____

_____

_____

_____

Explore and Experience

Are there any places I would like to visit and experiences I would like to have, either for the first time or again?

_____

_____

_____

_____

_____

_____

When will I make these dreams come true?

Consider making a more detailed to-do and action list to meet these goals. Your dreams will more likely come true!

_____

_____

_____

_____

_____

_____

Is there any way I want to change or deepen my spiritual life and awareness in these years?

As mentioned earlier, spirituality is not limited to religion and can be experienced profoundly through deepening our connection with our own soul, with nature, and with others.

_____

_____

_____

_____

Checking In

The Body

What is the general feeling, tone, and experience of my physical body during this time? Some examples include healthy, vibrant, beautiful, fragile, awkward/ugly, weak/insufficient, unstable, damaged, or an obstacle. There could be a combination of experiences.

_____

_____

_____

_____

If my body had a voice, what would it want to tell me?

If you've experienced physical issues, consider having a more extended back and forth dialogue with the "voices" of these parts of your body.

_____

_____

_____

_____

_____

What do I want to say to my body?

_____

_____

_____

_____

_____

The Heart

How is my physical heart doing?

_____
_____
_____
_____
_____
_____

What am I feeling? Do I yearn for any person or experience? Is my heart happy or sad? What brings me joy? What makes me sad?

_____
_____
_____
_____
_____
_____

If my heart had a voice, what would it want to tell me?

_____
_____
_____
_____
_____
_____

What do I want to tell my heart?

_____
_____

_____

_____

_____

_____

The Mind

How about my mind? What is the general tenor of my thoughts as I experience elderhood?

Examples might include excited/stimulated, creative, depressed, etc.

_____

_____

_____

_____

_____

_____

Grief

Loss is a real issue at this time of life, and grief accompanies loss. Grief honors loss. But it should not paralyze you indefinitely. Seek help if your depression, anxiety, and/or social isolation lasts longer than is healthy. Jewish tradition marks one year as the maximum time to absent yourself from life. That tradition marks gradual stages of reengagement in life throughout that year. Grief groups are hugely effective in helping to manage the grief from the losses that often accompany our elder years.

If you are suffering from extended anxiety or depression, please do not put off consulting your physician. Be especially aware of drug interactions and make sure your physician knows exactly what you are taking, including herbal remedies. Negative drug interactions can contribute to both anxiety and depression and can even result in death. Don't hide information from your physician.

Memory and Aging

Using the mind regularly keeps the brain in shape. Reading, solving puzzles, memorizing, learning a new skill, picking up or improving knowledge of another language, instrument or sport, attending dance classes, etc., discovering new places, all these examples stretch the mind. Being open to new learning along with exercise, good nutrition, enough sleep, and less stress, all help the brain to function well. Give love to the body and the mind.

Some loss of short-term memory is not uncommon, but interestingly, long-term memory typically becomes sharper. I believe there is a good reason for this. It may not just be a sign of dysfunction. At this stage, our memory seems to be focused on gathering memories of our lives from early on and sorting through them, much like the process of writing a memoir. Our short-term memory, like remembering the location of our keys, may no longer be as dependable, but there are practical solutions to those smaller problems. Meanwhile, your mind is taking on the bigger and more important task of reviewing your life's journey, determining who mattered and what.

Am I using my mind to learn and experience new things? What keeps my mind and my life fresh?

_____

_____

_____

_____

_____

_____

What do I find myself thinking about when I am not focusing on a task?

_____

_____

_____

_____

_____

_____

Do any memories from the past keep recurring? Which Ones?

_____

_____

_____

_____

_____

_____

_____

Do they need processing? What can I do to better integrate those experiences?

In depth journaling, letter writing (there are letters that can be sent and others that should not be sent, but are ways to find resolution none the less), ritual, creative expression, talking with a trained counselor, psychotherapist are ways to consider working through past material.

_____

_____

_____

_____

_____

_____

_____

The Spirit

What is my relationship to spirituality at this time in my life? Has it shifted from earlier years? If so, how? Where and in what way do I experience spirituality?

_____

_____

_____

_____

_____

_____

_____

Are there any ways I want to change or deepen my spiritual life and awareness?

_____

_____

_____

_____

_____

What would my soul like to tell me about this stage in my life?

_____

_____

_____

_____

_____

A Good Death

Facing the inevitability of death and regarding the end of this life as natural is fundamental to a growing respect for our elders and for our own eldering. It's equally as important for living a good life in whatever stage we're in.

Disconnection from nature has led to a linear view of life, in which death is viewed as the final act. More traditional cultures, however, ones that are more attuned to nature, have always regarded death not as an end but as part of an ongoing cycle. Rituals were in place to honor the body, envisioning the essence of the person, the soul, returning to the spirit world, or the "realm of the ancestors."

Life within the family also created a broader context, more inclusive of life and death, with multiple generations living together and providing support for the older members. Often members were born and died within the family home or compound. With greater mobility and an emphasis on the individual and the nuclear family, that support structure has crumbled. The threat of loneliness, isolation, and physical vulnerability have heightened the terror of aging and death, as well as the struggle to keep up the appearance of youth.

Thankfully, movements are under way to bring back respect for the aging person and the process of moving into and through the final stages of this life. Many new options are being explored that can help facilitate the passage for the dying person. Psilocybin, in the proper amount can transform fear to an experience of beauty, oneness, and a trusting surrender. For the remaining family, friends, and community, more meaningful ceremonies are being created.

The huge profiteering in many of the mortuary businesses, trading on people's grief and fear, is coming to light. Much more affordable and ecological options are becoming available that offer both dignity and respect to the souls of those who have passed and the souls of those who remain.

Heavy metal caskets as well as common methods of cremation are not environmentally clean solutions to burial. Some resources for this information, including laws that vary in the U.S. from state to state, are offered in the Tools section at the end of this workbook. In many places, the laws regarding burial options are changing as a growing activist movement becomes more visible. The ways we navigate our elder years, and the dying process are slowly undergoing a needed renaissance. Ancient traditions are being recovered, and new ones are being created that are more honoring and therapeutic for our elders, the dying, and the living who are left behind.

Do I have a spiritual/philosophical perspective about death? Am I able to find peace in my perspective?

If you are a humanist, or adhere to philosophic "naturalism," these count as spiritual perspectives. Spirituality is a far more inclusive term than religion.

_____

_____

_____

_____

_____

_____

_____

_____

Indigenous tribes worldwide have a close affinity with the earth and the natural world. Though there is the loss of the human being, there is a view that the Earth takes the body back into herself, like the mother she is to all her creatures. Extremely ancient burial sites often reveal bodies lying in the fetal position, just as they did in their human mother's womb.

Death has been imagined as an archetype in many ways. Do you see death as an angel or as a mother taking you home? Or do you visualize the Grim Reaper or something else more frightening taking you into another realm? Do you imagine death as an empty void?

It has been suggested in metaphysics that the spiritual idea of a guardian angel (an invisible being offering lifelong guidance and protection) is the one who will escort us at the end of our story.

How do I envision death?

_____

_____

_____

_____

If I have a frightening view of death, is it possible for me to imagine it differently? Could my views of death as scary be the result of cultural fears of aging and death? What view of death can serve me rather than scare me?

_____

_____

_____

_____

_____

_____

Do I feel ready to let go when the time comes? If not, what still needs to be processed or healed?

_____

_____

_____

_____

_____

_____

_____

_____

On a Practical Level

How best can I prepare for my death? Have I made a legal Will and assigned Trusts, Power of Attorney, and Advance Directive forms?

_____

_____

_____

_____

_____

_____

_____

Does my family know where to find my documents and passwords so they can access any needed information regarding my estate?

_____

_____

_____

_____

What do I want to happen with my body? Have I let my family know?

_____

_____

_____

_____

Do I want a funeral or celebration? If so, how would I like that to be?

_____

_____

_____

_____

_____

_____

Who do I imagine attending?

_____

_____

_____

_____

_____

_____

To conclude, I offer this poem by the Irish/English poet, David Whyte:

Beyond Santiago

Death is so simple,
one moment
you are alive
and then,
you are not.

And that fear
you carry with you
might be
equally as simple too,

that you'll
never have
the time
to accomplish
what you wish.

But stop
a moment now,
before the way
beyond,
and let me
tell you this.

You will go
out of this life
however
untimely,
having completed
every single thing
you wished.

You will
arrive
in that night like
a newborn child
welcomed
by
loving arms.

You will find
in that long
anticipated
enemy,
the ultimate form
of forgiveness
and
friendship.

Every
fearful goodbye
suddenly become,
a gentle
getting to know,

a getting to know
of a forgiveness
that was strangely
always anticipated,
a welcome
and a full understanding
of all you ever did,

everything you gave
and everything
you were given,
and then everything
you could never give,
and above all
everything you
could never
bring yourself
to receive,

those unattainable
distances
that always
broke your heart
and the gifted
understanding
of why it was so hard
for you to love,

and then
and most importantly
and right to the heart,

everything you were
and everything you gave,
that was never,
ever on your list.[1]

1. David Whyte, "Beyond Santiago," from *David Whyte: Still Possible*, @ 2022. David Whyte, Reprinted with permission from David Whyte and Many Rivers Company, LLC, Langley, WA. www.davidwhyte.com.

Putting It All Together

Mythic Themes

Are you able to find any classic themes from traditional or contemporary tales and myths in your story? Do you relate to a particular hero, heroine, s/hero? Maybe you relate to the ancient and more modern versions of seers and shamans, some of whom travel both the path of masculine and feminine. Alternatively, do you resonate with a more mysterious and ambiguous character like Severus Snape in Harry Potter?[1]

Anti-heroes, too, play a valuable role in the bigger story of humanity. You might have had the task of being a truth teller to an unreceptive or defensive audience. Your role may have been as an alchemizer, bringing light into a very dark and resistant reality. You may be a person whose calling has been to question the status quo, expanding people's perceptions and challenging their limited views. Or maybe, at times, you played the villain, paradoxically encouraging another person to step into their power. Without the challenger or the challenge, there is no real story! Look for resonances between your life and traditional tales.

As humans, we all participate in a shared psychological field that transcends time. We each tend to reflect larger human stories in our personal lives. The bigger stories *are* our stories. Traditional stories and myths like Snow White and Sleeping Beauty, as well as the myths of Psyche, Persephone, and Ariadne are depictions of a young girl's evolution from maiden to woman.

Maybe your life has some resonance to the benevolent fairy godmother? Or have you found yourself in the role of the evil stepmother, ultimately encouraging someone to step into their power and sovereignty through your tough love. Perhaps you feel a kinship with the complex figure of Morgan Le Fay in the Arthurian legends. The masculine figures in these tales represent the development of the woman's inner compliment, the "animus," and the evolution of finding a balance between her femininity and inner masculinity.

The same can be said in reverse for a boy. The females within these stories represent the inner feminine, or "anima." Many boys have felt the call to adventure and resonate, for example, with the stories of the Quest for the Holy Grail in the

1. S/hero is used here to include those who identify as non-binary.

adventures of the Arthurian knights. More contemporary examples are young Frodo and the brave Baromir, or the magician Gandalf of J.R.R. Tolkien's trilogy, The Lord of the Rings. Alternatively, you might have played an anti-hero for a time, acitng out the bully that awakened courage and strength in another.

Non-binary folk can find resonance with Kapaemahu and the Mahu ancestors of Polynesian myths, Tiresius of Greek Myth, and the stories of many indigenous shamans worldwide. One native American story, a true one in fact, is the life of We'wha, a Zuni, and the most famous berdache (an individual who combined the work and traits of both men and women) in American history. Gender-bending figures exist, too, in Norse, Greek, Hindu, and many other world mythologies.

We are each a hologram of the larger story. Yet we are not simple replicas. Each of us expresses the bigger story through the distinctive lens of our own expression. To understand that we are one with humanity and still add a precious, unique expression to this life is so important. Both are true.

Just as we live in a paradoxical reality that asks us to balance opposites, spiritual teachers and sages have told us that the Divine is transcendent as well as immanent, and that we are children of the stars and spirit, as well as the earth and the body. Physicists have discovered the paradox of wave and particle expressions of light. We are presented here with the deeper truth, which is that we cannot simply divide anyone or anything into one category or another. There is no indelible "other."

It's vital that we come to see our uniqueness as well as our shared journey, our common heritage. Accepting and then harmonizing these differences within our own personalities helps us harmonize with the differences we encounter in others. This is how peace begins, both personal peace and world peace.

The following prompts shed light on the deeper meaning and purpose you might find within your life's story.

What stories (myths, legends, fairy tales, novels, screenplays, etc.) come to mind that feel as if they are my story, at least in part?

_____

_____

_____

_____

_____

What characters do I identify with and why?

If you had a narcissistic mother or step-mother, maybe you identify with Snow White. Maybe you identify with Cinderella if you had difficult relationships with your siblings or were made to do the unpleasant tasks in your family home.

Another example might be the story of Parsifal, a boy who had to disengage from his mother so he would be able to test himself and grow into his manhood.

Maybe you've felt like the orphan in the story of the poor little match girl or Mowgli in Rudyard Kipling's novel or Harry Potter.

Have you been a modern day "Robin Hood," defending the poor?

Have you been the unpopular truth teller, like Casandra in Greek tragedy; have you been sorely misjudged and persecuted by others after making heroic sacrifices like Joan of Arc or Prometheus?

These are just a few examples. Who do you relate to and why?

_____

_____

_____

_____

_____

_____

Who have been the important supporting characters in my life? How did they affect my journey?

Think of supportive people who have helped you get to where you are today. How so?

_____

_____

_____

_____

_____

Who have played the role of the antagonist in my story? How did they affect my jourmey?

List those who have played the adversary in your life and consider how they played a role in the trajectory of your life.

_____

_____

_____

_____

_____

_____

There may have been people who both supported *and* challenged you. Name them here and describe how they acted out each role in your life.

_____

_____

_____

_____

_____

_____

_____

_____

What opposing forces did I have to face, both externally and internally?

Examples might include poverty, war, exile, prejudice, etc.

_____

_____

_____

_____

_____

_____

_____

_____

How did these opposing forces help me grow?

_____

_____

_____

_____

_____

_____

What key experiences—conflicts and losses, as well as successes and triumphs—
have most impacted me and defined my life?

_____

_____

_____

_____

_____

_____

_____

_____

_____

_____

_____

What choices did I make, or were made for me, that have strongly influenced the direction of my life?

_____

_____

_____

_____

_____

_____

_____

_____

Following the threads, what circumstances or choices led to what outcome?

Sometimes what seems like a chance meeting or a random choice led to a significant turn in the road of your life. This question is a big one and will likely take more than the lines offered here. Get out your journal to continue your answer if needed.

_____

_____

_____

_____

_____

_____

_____

_____

_____

_____

In each part of this workbook, we have explored themes woven through your story. Review those themes, add any new ones you discover, and record below.

_____

_____

_____

_____

_____

_____

_____

What patterns do you notice in your story? What repetitive experiences showed up in your life, under new guises, and expressions.

Examples of positive patterns might be last-minute rescue in dangerous moments, being lucky in finding love, work, housing, or the right teacher, being in the right place at the right time, etc.

_____

_____

_____

_____

_____

_____

_____

_____

_____

Examples of negative patterns might be losing a coveted and anticipated opportunity several times in life, being falsely accused or betrayed more than once, etc.

_____

_____

_____

_____

_____

_____

_____

_____

_____

What traits and strengths have I developed through my lifetime of experience that weren't as strong when I was a child?

Maybe you overcame fears? Which ones? Maybe you learned perseverance, discipline, empathy, loyalty, courage etc.?

_____

_____

_____

_____

_____

Earlier in this workbook you identified what you have learned about yourself, your preferences, your core values, and what is most important to you. These are important aspects of the hero/heroine/s/hero of your story. List them again here:

My core values are:

_____

_____

_____

_____

_____

_____

_____

_____

_____

In just a few words, in essence, answer these questions:

What have been my prevailing archetypes?

Examples include warrior, nurturer, healer, priest/priestess, teacher, guide, mentor, leader, artist, creator, initiator, alchemizer, translator, visionary, lover, mediator, harmonizer, truth teller, etc. Feel free to make up your own.

Maybe you have embodied different archetypes at different periods in your life. What have they been?

_____

_____

_____

_____

_____

_____

_____

From Carbon to Diamond, From Lead to Gold

Earlier in our review, you were asked to consider the "shadow" qualities of your parents. The example offered was one parent abused their power and the other displayed overly narcissistic tendencies. Ideally, the child of these parents is eventually able to claim healthy power and self-love—the most positive expressions of these shadow qualities. This is an example, there are many other possibilities.

The innate strengths and weaknesses of our primary caregivers form the rough elements we're given coming into this life. Perhaps your soul wanted to experiment with these traits—these primary ingredients, your *prima materia* in this life. Maybe you have spent many years polishing these genetic and spiritual parts of yourself. If you have, then it's likely you feel a wholeness, peace and an inner freedom.

But if you haven't experimented with polishing the rough elements into jewels, it's not too late to begin. The formula is to find the qualities of your caregivers that were most detrimental to you, qualities that you instinctively distanced yourself from. It is likely that you encountered these qualities again and again in different people playing the same roles on your journey. Turn to face these qualities and find the hidden virtue in their distorted expressions, and you will find the jewels in the cave of the dragon. Claiming them in their positive expression adds great richness to life.

Alchemy is a circular and circulating process of distancing, separating, and reuniting. It is a continuing upward spiral of evolution, with the goal of beautifully harmonizing the ingredients. Your life is an opportunity to produce the alchemical gems of maturity.

In the space below, consider how you have worked with the rough stones of your childhood. Have these hidden gems been handed to you repeatedly throughout your life, much like the recurring themes and patterns you detected throughout your journey? Have you polished what you received into shining gems? If not, how might you allow this work to move forward?

_____

_____

_____

_____

_____

_____

_____

_____

_____

_____

_____

_____

In what other ways have you grown personally, including how you have overcome patterns in your extended ancestral heritage?

_____

_____

_____

_____

_____

_____

_____

_____

_____

_____

_____

Where do I feel I am in the alchemical process of my life? What feels like it still needs work?

How would I still like to grow?

_____

_____

_____

_____

_____

_____

_____

My Alchemical Journey: Part Four

Consider the big picture of your life as you write the conclusion of your alchemical journey. Consider who you were when you arrived in an infant body and how you have transformed through the years. Remember the lives you have touched and whose lives have touched yours. Just by being born, you have impacted others and the world. You just being you has had an impact. You have made a difference.

You may have had notable achievements, or your life might have been a quiet one. Likely you've caused damage to others (we all have), and to yourself at times, but that, too, has been an offering and made a mark. Possibly what you view as your mistakes or harmful actions or inactions have prompted growth in another. How have you grown and evolved? The purpose of this final part of your story is to acknowledge this big picture. If you want to change things, you are still here and there is still time.

Consider what you have loved and who you have loved. As Irish/English poet David Whyte points out, what and who you have loved, more than your accomplishments, define the Presence you are and who you have been in this world. Love is the ultimate "alchemizer!"

In the following space, continue your story, from the perspective of the alchemist. If you have not lived your elder years yet, imagine the story as you would like it to unfold. What have you (or hope to have) transformed, transmuted and created in the laboratory of your soul?

_____

_____

_____

_____

_____

_____

_____

_____

_____

You have been writing your story your whole life. Now it's time for the larger Truth: You are *not* your story. In the end, you will release it. You have traveled the Wheel of Life, experiencing and experimenting along the way. At the end of this story, you will be released from the Wheel.

Buddhism offers a powerful image of the wheel we enter when we are born into this world. The mandala of The Wheel of Life is divided into six "Lokas," or states of consciousness. We can discover ourselves in any one of these and reside there for quite a long time, feeling trapped. Some states are more tempting to live in than others. The six realms include the "hell" realm of anger and hatred, the "hungry ghost" realm of greed, the "animal" realm of fear, as well as the realms of jealousy, ignorance, and complacency.

The good news is that we are not bound to any one of these realms. The goal of growth is to be fully in this life while being able to disentangle ourselves from these emotional states of mind and heart. Because of consciousness, we can make a new choice about where we want to reside on this wheel as soon as we notice we're hooked. And we can alchemize our experiences into something nourishing to the soul and for the world. At the end of your life's story, you will be invited to free yourself from the wheel. The work you have done here has contributed to that freedom.

Now it's time to celebrate you! To celebrate the work and play of "Gnothi Seauton,"[1] that most valuable pursuit of all, the real effort to "know yourself."

Through challenges, risks, failures, and successes, you have traveled an often winding and sometimes treacherous road. What a story! By your willingness and effort to engage in this workbook, you are a person who is endeavoring to live a conscious life. You are a Light in a world often shrouded in darkness.

Our world will only find balance and peace if we each do our work. You are so valuable in healing us and our Earth. Thank you for your courage and your beauty.

It's time to celebrate *you* and a job well done!

1. *Gnothi Seuton* ("Know Thyself") is the Greek inscription on the Temple of Apollo and Dionysos at Delphi.

TOOLS FOR DEEPENING & METHODS OF HEALING

Alchemy

Further references on alchemy:

The Emerald Tablet: Alchemy for Personal Transformation, Dennis William Hauck.

An in-depth view of applying alchemy and its stages to the growth of consciousness.

The author gives his own life experiences as an example.

The Anatomy of the Psyche: Alchemical Symbolism in Psychotherapy, Edward F. Edinger.

A Jungian book by psychiatrist and renowned Jungian analyst describing alchemical stages in psychotherapy as witnessed through symbols in the client's dreams and fantasies.

Alchemy, The Secret Art, Stanislas Klossowski de Rola.

A richly illustrated scholarly introduction to alchemy.

The Dictionary of Alchemical Imagery. Lyndy Abraham.

Difficult to find but excellent dictionary of alchemical language and imagery.

The Encyclopedia of Dreams, Symbols and Interpretations, Rosemary Ellen Guiley.

A useful dictionary of the symbolism found in dreams through an alchemical lens.

Building Self Esteem

The Barbie Mirror Exercise

When my daughter was a little girl, sometime in the late 1990s, she was given a Barbie mirror as a present—a three-sided vanity mirror framed by Barbie's signature pink plastic, with a button you could push to hear Barbie's voice cheering you on. Through the mirror, Barbie would tell you, "You look great!" "You're my best friend!" "You're Awesome," etc.

Twenty years ago, I told my best friend, Lorraine (mentioned in the Preface as the inspiration for this workbook), about this mirror and how I had been personally struggling with confidence.

Just before I flew home from a visit with her, she handed me a sealed envelope with a drawing of a hand mirror on it, addressed to me. She told me not to open it until I got on the plane. Buckled into my seat after takeoff, I opened the envelope and found a long list of all the things she loved about me and respected. It was an amazing and unexpected gift that meant the world to me when I was in a very difficult period of my life. That is how the Barbie Mirror exercise was born.

When you deeply need a boost of confidence, ask someone you love and trust, someone who knows you well, to write a Barbie Mirror letter for you. Maybe you can give them one in return, or write one for a friend who is feeling alone and needing a boost. Let them know what you love and appreciate about them. You will know when that is the right thing.

We tend to remember criticisms better than praise. Hypnotherapy explains this tendency as a purposeful and protective design. The negative experiences are bold in our memory to serve as warnings in the future. However, this emphasis on the negative tends to minimize, and even erase from conscious memory, the positive reflections we receive from others. In the lines below, write the great things people have told you about you! Review and add to it from time to time.

_____

_____

_____

_____

———————————————————————
———————————————————————
———————————————————————
———————————————————————
———————————————————————
———————————————————————

A Celebration Notebook

You can also consider keeping a celebration notebook—a book in which you write the compliments you receive and the "wins," both small and large, that you experience. Practice receiving and savoring this praise, not deflecting it.

If you've had critical people in your life, you might have learned to defend yourself by anticipating criticism and inflicting it upon yourself in preparation for an attack from the outside. Being able to receive praise is a courageous act. It requires a softening that can feel quite vulnerable. But the reward of this courage are tremendous. You will, perhaps for the first time, be able to see the incredible traits you bring into this world. This world needs your unique light, and we need you to own it.

Journaling

I have journaled nearly every morning for over forty years. For me, this practice has been the best way to keep in touch with my own process, to listen to the wisdom of my dreams, and to work out how best to respond—and not simply react—to what comes in life. Journaling is my number one suggestion for anyone who wants to continue the self-reflective work we've done in this workbook. Through consistent journaling, we can live a more conscious and considered life.

If you like to write by hand, then find a journal you really love, one that feels honoring of your most intimate and precious work. If you prefer to write on your computer, dedicate a special folder to this journal. You can name that folder anything, especially if privacy is an issue, but having a dedicated space for your honest thoughts and feelings is important.

Dreams can be recorded or quickly scrawled onto a piece of paper in the night. In the morning, you have something to work with in your journal. Even a single remembered image can lead to some very rich results.

Listening to Your Intuition, the Small Still Voice

Your inner knowing is your greatest ally. How many times have you had a niggling doubt but you pushed through it, doing or saying something, or trusting that person anyway, only to regret it later? We all have. Intuitive knowledge can appear in bodily messages (a gut feeling, a feeling of contraction of the heart, a sense of coldness, a weakening of the knees, or a stubbed toe, etc.). Sometimes, it's just a knowing deep inside that you can't explain. It can show up in synchronicities and speak through dreams.

Learning to quiet the mind and listen to your intuition is an art in this outwardly focused, driven world. While our conscious mind may be neutral or have another opinion about a situation, a deeper part of us whispers the best direction. Almost, if not always, we later realize that voice was correct.

The voice of intuition as guidance will never put you down or threaten you. It is a "still small voice" that Knows, beyond appearances and reason. It is there to steer you toward your smoothest path of evolution. If you ignore it, you still have the opportunity for growth. But it might be a long detour to recover the direct route forward. Still, inevitably, we learn and grow.

The practices of mindfulness, somatic awareness, meditation, journaling, dream work, and breath work are all routes to create a more conscious connection with these intuitive messages.

The Body as our Faithful Advisor

The body is the surest barometer we have. While we may delude ourselves from conscious or unconscious motives, the body does not lie. When we become sensitive to its responses, our body becomes a powerful ally and tool for deciphering ourselves and our experiences. This is why muscle testing works. It bypasses the rational mind and questions the body instead.

The Focusing Method is a technique described and practiced by therapist Eugene Gendlin, who collaborated early on in his career with Humanistic psychologist Carl Rogers. I have used the Focusing technique and taught it to clients throughout my many years of practice. It has inevitably produced astoundingly quick results and benefits.

The Focusing Method

1) Consider an issue that is troubling you.
2) Find where you feel it in your body. Stay with that feeling, softening your awareness, while resting it in the place of discomfort.
3) With your attention localized at that place, consider if you can associate the feeling with an image or felt sense. What color, shape, weight is it?
4) Describe the feeling to yourself as best you can as you stay with it. Whatever comes, comes. don't force.
5) For several minutes, be with that place and the feeling in the body, identifying its qualities.
6) Listen. What is it saying? What does it need? What is this place asking for?
7) Visualize giving what that place in body and the imagination is asking for. You might "see" what could bring that place relief. Sometimes this involves visualizing spaciousness in the area and sometimes a different color arriving etc. What will bring that place comfort?
8) Watch what occurs. Give it some time. Is there a shift? Very often, there is, and with it comes a sense of relief. It's as if the body has just been waiting for your attentive listening. That relief most often gives rise to a way forward out of the stuckness.
9) If you don't feel a shift yet, check in from time to time. Be patient with that place and with yourself.

Attending your soul as it speaks through your body and through the imagination is valuable work. It loosens our stuck places. Often, we can't see clearly to respond to life's events because of something that has gotten lodged in us from our past, and even the past of our ancestors. Loosening these places up, lovingly, allows us to be available to life here and now. Uncontaminated by old traumas, our decisions in the present are far better too.

Self-Expression

Art and Dance

Art and dance are beautiful ways to process our feelings. You do not need to be an artist or a good dancer to do this work. Both are private expressions that let your psyche know you are interested in what it has to say and want to honor that relationship. Allowing a feeling to move through your hands and feet acts as an integration, healing the separation we often experience between the outer world and our inner life.

Reverence and Gratitude Practices

Prayer and Meditation

Prayer is talking with Spirit, however we imagine it. Prayer can include gratitude, petition, or simply remembrance of our connection with the Sacred.

Meditation is listening. It quiets our rambling thoughts, our preoccupation with the outer world and its tasks. In meditation we focus our attention inward. It can be done as a practice of thought witnessing, in which we allow our thoughts to come and go without holding onto them.

In many forms of meditation, we focus on connecting with our deep core self, an experience often described as pure nondual awareness. In this state, there is no identity, simply unity with all that is. We no longer focus on past or future, we are entirely in the present. This experience is often described as pure bliss.

The Eternal has been called Spirit, God/Goddess, or even "The Universe." It is both transcendent and right here with us. It is objective and at the same time, the most intimate. Beyond all the shifting of identities, time and space, It *is* us. Our meditation practice just brings us "home."

Gratitude

Gratitude has a powerfully positive effect on the quality of our lives. A daily practice of remembering what we are grateful for lifts our mood and our energetic frequency, helping relieve our anxiety and depression. A gratitude list before bed, in the morning, or any time of day, creates a more peaceful state and positive connection with life.

The Importance of Ritual

We perform rituals every day, from making our daily cup of tea or coffee and brushing our teeth, to yearly rituals for holidays and special celebrations. Creating a ritual to mark a desired or accomplished change can serve as a powerful focus of our intention.

The cycles of the moon are supportive foundations for this practice. On new moons, write what you would like to release on one strip of paper. On another piece, write what you would like to grow during the coming month.

To release what you've written on the first piece of paper, burn it in fireproof bowl on one of the several days of the dark balsamic moon just before the new crescent. Dispose of the ashes in a way that feels right for you.

Keep the other piece of paper in a special place (on your "altar," if you have one), This serves as a reminder of your goals, as you travel the next two weeks toward the full moon. On the full moon, you can decide to keep or burn the list as a prayer of thanksgiving for their actualization.

Consider whether you have you seen any progress? Rituals activate the unconscious in support of our conscious intentions.

Visioning Your Future

Creating a Vision Board of desired goals and intentions is a powerful way of engaging the subconscious mind through images. The subconscious relates far more readily to pictures and felt sensation than to words.

Consider what you would like to manifest and the feelings you would like to feel in the future. Find images (on the internet, in magazines, etc.) that evoke the feelings and experiences you want to bring into your life.

Create a collage with the images on a poster board. You can add words or phrases if they help to increase your felt desire. Place the collage in a place where you will see it in the morning when you wake and before you go to sleep. Wait for the magic! Of course, you need to do what you can to help those visions become reality. Image plus feeling plus action create.

Relationships

Cultivating Relationship with Nature and with Each Other

Relationships impact our integrity. If we perceive one another as objects, it is very easy to lie, cheat, steal, and murder. War becomes acceptable and even inevitable. If we consider the earth as something to be manipulated for what she can produce, we have no sense of her living spirit or the reciprocity involved in a real relationship. If we are "in relationship" with the world around us, it is far less likely that we can harm, pollute or destroy without some feeling and a sense of responsibility.

In cultivating relationship, we experience everyone and everything as connected to us, a part of a larger whole. Each part of the whole is entitled to respect and reciprocity. When we hurt another, or the land, we hurt ourselves. Becoming awake to a shared system, we step into responsible participation in life.

Indigenous cultures know how to read nature. They had to do so for survival. All of us were indigenous once. People who are connected to the land know how to open and extend awareness to "the voices" of plants and animals, and even to the mineral kingdoms. They know how to read the weather along with phases of the moon, stars, and sun. Those "voices," through signs and signatures, speak to them, teaching what is healthful and helpful to humans and what is dangerous and possibly deadly. This conversation is only possible through cultivating relationships with these beings.

Once upon a time, we all understood we were part of nature and there was no separation. Nature has always been our teacher and our cocreator. She is not an object for us to dominate, and we do so to our detriment. Our health and the health of our planet depends on us relating to her as a living, feeling being of which we are a part and with whom we can dialogue and cooperate. Finally, we enrich our own lives cultivating relationship with nature and with each other.

Freeing Yourself for Good from a Toxic Relationship

When you have been in a close toxic relationship with a lover or friend, you may get the courage to end it but be tempted repeatedly to return. Relationships can act like a rubber band. We distance but then we feel a powerful pull to return. Relationships create subtle invisible strings tying us to one another despite our best intentions. They can feel incredibly hard to break even when we know we are psychically and even sometimes physically in danger.

Create a list of reasons why you are leaving. If it feels right, put that list in a "Don't Forget" journal. Pull out this list and re-read every time you feel the temptation to return. Consider if you feel in your gut whether the person really has changed. Your heart and your mind can become confused, but your gut knows. Often you will just know, despite appearances, you would be returning to the same toxic situation, only to have to leave all over again. With enough time, the rubber band does break, and you will be free. You will wonder how you stayed as long as you did.

Healing Trauma

Resources:

Books

What Happened to You? Conversations on Trauma, Resilience, and Healing
Bruce D. Perry, M.D.., Ph.D., Oprah Winfrey

The Body Keeps the Score
Bessel Van der Kolk, M.D.

Healing Trauma
Peter Levine

Somatic Experiencing as a Powerful Resource for Trauma Release

Somatic work focuses on our bodies and sees them as expressions of our energy. Our bodies carry our trauma; they are acutely aware of our thoughts and our emotional experiences. Trained practitioners in somatic work can compassionately release trauma from our bodies, allowing energy to flow freely once again.

Healing Generational Trauma – The Constellation Work of Bert Hellinger

Bert Hellinger was raised in a Germany that demanded complete submissiveness to the State at all costs—Nazi Germany. It encouraged neighbors to betray neighbors, friends to betray friends, and children to betray parents if there was any question of loyalty to the regime. Hellinger witnessed the atrocities committed both by the Nazis and the allies in their treatment of prisoners. War seemed to absolve people of their humanity, and unbending adherence to an ideology devastated millions of lives.

After the war, Hellinger entered the Catholic priesthood and served as a missionary in Africa. He lived sixteen years with the Zulu in Africa. A strong antagonist to apartheid, he greatly admired the Zulu. He witnessed their deep respect for their ancestors and their belief in their presence after death. In stark contrast to the propaganda of Hellinger's youth, the Zulu saw the betrayal of family as an unthinkable act.

Their sensitivity planted the seeds for his future work. When Hellinger was asked whether he would support the ideals of the Church over the people he served and their situations, Hellinger found he was unable to continue as a Catholic priest. Upholding the ideals of the Church at any cost to the people became untenable. Just as he struggled with the dictates of the Nazi regime, Hellinger's conscience could no longer allow him to represent a religious organization that demanded unquestioning obedience to an ideology and its representatives.

Returning to Germany and having left the priesthood, he began an intensive study of psychology and emerging healing methods. In addition to the more traditional methods, he studied Milton Erickson's hypnotherapy, the Family Systems and the Family Sculpture method of Virginia Satir, the Primal Scream therapy of Arthur Janov, and the Transactional Analysis Method with Eric Berne.

He noted that young Germans who were born after the war into a restored and thriving economy, a vast contrast to war-torn Germany, were exhibiting the same trauma characteristics and responses as their parents and grandparents who had gone through the war. His experience with the Zulu, combined with his studies, gave birth to his method of trauma relief: Constellation Therapy.

Nurture, of course, has its influence, but science (excepting the newer studies in epigenetics) has no explanation for the recurrence of the same method of suicide on the same day of the year two generations apart by a descendent who had never met his uncle and had not been told of the suicide. These two men were also in the same birth order of the family. I am not inventing this example. It comes from my own family. I discovered this coincidence when I created a family genogram with the help of my mother before she died.

Neither the Zulu nor Hellinger would be surprised. They believe we carry forward the unhealed wounds of our ancestors, and without intervention the trauma response will repeat itself in us, as ancient tradition teaches, to the seventh generation (and perhaps beyond).

How Does Constellation Therapy Work?

Most often this work is carried out in a group. The client presents an issue for the group to work on, for example, repeated rejection, betrayal or abuse. The facilitating therapist will then ask the client to choose specific participants to embody the roles of their various family members.

Wordlessly, the client moves the players into the positions that represent how they tended to relate to one another in the family. Sometimes even aborted babies and those who left the family are represented in this exercise and put into position in relationship to the group. No information is offered other than who the participants are and their relative positions. No family history is provided, even to the therapist.

The therapist then poses questions to the actors to discover what each is feeling and thinking from their position. The answers are inevitably shockingly correct to the client. The therapist then determines how to move the players and if more actors are needed to fill the roles of ancestors further back. Eventually a change in positions invites reconciliation and a therapeutic resolution, liberating the client as well as future generations from the ancestral trauma wound.

I have witnessed and personally participated in this work. I have referred many clients to this therapeutic approach. Invariably, there have been successful results. The work seems to employ a sort of telepathy, using what Rupert Sheldrake calls "the morphogenetic field" of resonance. There is no overt information passed except the positioning of the participants. Yet they seem to intuitively know the thoughts and feelings of the ancestors and how they have related to one another. It is more than a spatial positioning of the clients. The actors seem to know more than what possibly could be deduced simply by positioning. A skilled facilitator knows how to direct the action toward revelation and then healing.

The Zulus would not question this, nor would any indigenous culture that considers the dead a living legacy and continued presence in the tribe or clan. In indigenous belief, the ancestors are still carrying pain and waiting for the next generation to heal them both. Almost everyone has a generationally inherited experience of trauma. Positive results have been achieved using this modern but ancient technique in the treatment of anxiety disorders, depression, PTSD, excessive anger, and addiction.

Healing Shame

David Bedrick's "Unshaming" work.
www.davidbedrick.com

Brené Brown's many books and videos.
www.brenébrown.com

When We Leave

Someday it will be time to end this story, our personal story. If we are still conscious during the dying process, it is very likely that our actions or inactions will come forward for reckoning in our own mind. I have been with the dying and witnessed this firsthand. Becoming conscious and accountable now, before that time, will vastly improve the quality of our life in the present as well as our death when it arrives. If we can leave as cleanly as we can, with no mess left behind, our hearts will weigh less than Ma'at's feather on the scale of justice. The scale of justice weighs for balance. What we leave unfinished behind us is an imbalance, and that imbalance affects the generations that follow.

Finally...A Sense of Humor

Remember to see the comedy in the dramas we create in our human experience. It has been said that you will know the devil by his lack of mirth. Being able to laugh at life and at ourselves can not only save us from a deep dive into depression, but it is also a sign of maturity. As author and coach Michael Larsen points out, "The more you laugh, the more open you are to learning."

MORE TOOLS FOR SELF AWARENESS

Personality Inventories

There is no shortage of personality inventories. Personality inventories are tools to help pinpoint your strengths and your particular approach to life. Below is a list to get you started.

The Myers-Briggs Inventory

This inventory is based on Jung's division of personality types into the varying strengths of four functions: Thinking, Feeling, Sensation, and Intuition. These categories have specific definitions in Jungian psychology. Two functions will be found to be most dominant in a person while the third less so and the fourth typically underdeveloped. In Jungian thought, it is our life task to ultimately strengthen the third and the final fourth function to achieve a more whole expression of ourselves. A tendency toward extroversion vs. introversion is included in this analysis tool as well.

There are multiple offerings that include Myers-Briggs tests, descriptions of type and how to relate to people with differing types.

The Enneagram

The Enneagram is a system based on nine personality descriptions. One will be a dominant personality feature with an adjacent "wing" expression and, when in stress, a person acts from the less developed aspects of one other type.

These are some of the most comprehensive books on the Enneagram and how to utilize it:

The Wisdom of the Enneagram: The Complete Guide to Psychological and Spiritual Growth for the Nine Personality Types, Don Richard Riso and Russ Hudson.

The Enneagram, Understanding Yourself and Others in Your Life, Helen Palmer.

The Process Communication Model

In this model, each of us is a particular combination of six possible types: The Thinker, The Persister, The Harmonizer, The Imaginer, The Rebel, and The Promoter, with one type taking the lead. This inventory explores the differences in perception and goals of each. Like all of the inventories, the goal is to better understand yourself and others.

The Five Love Languages

This perspective offers a helpful assessment revealing how we show care for another person. We don't all show love in the same way. Knowing our differing Love Languages creates greater understanding and appreciation in couples, friends, and families.

A Human Design and The Gene Keys

This is a newer system combining astrology, the I Ching, Kabbalah and Vedic philosophy. It divides personalities into four types, describing how we exchange energy with the world. Types include Manifestors, Generators, Projectors, and Reflectors. Subtypes and specific gifts are attributed to your specific birthdate, time, and place. It is a complex but fascinating system.

Richard Rudd, a long-time student of A Human Design, has created *The Gene Keys*, a derivative system based mainly on the I Ching. This is an interesting path to continue study, if you are drawn to A Human Design.

Astrology

Astrology is a more complex and long-standing system that calculates the time and place of your birth in relationship to the position of the planets. Astrology has been practiced in many cultures worldwide for millennia, and by some of the brightest minds in history, including scientists who have been considered geniuses such as Kepler, Galileo and Brahe. While it has summarily been dismissed in favor of a more materialistic approach, its insight and allure has never died because it offers so much to those who seek out its wisdom.

When one comes from a systems and relational perspective, astrology seems entirely possible. Why wouldn't we be psychologically influenced by the cosmos? If all of nature, including us, is in relationship, then it isn't an impossible stretch to consider that we, too, are in relationship with our solar system and beyond, both physically and psychologically.

Gardeners and farmers have always calculated planting and harvesting according to solar and lunar phases. From an astrological perspective, the planets, including our own, are "bodies," both physical and subtle, having their own characteristics and influences, just as we do. "As above, so below," as the ancient hermetic principle teaches. If you have a soul-based view of reality, then astrology is a useful tool in understanding your life plan, i.e. who you came in as—your gifts as well as your challenges.

The position of the planets at the time of your birth, from the perspective of Earth, produces a map of your strengths and talents as well as areas that call for attention if you are to grow and evolve. A good birth chart reading can tell you a lot about yourself. Following the transits of planets as they influence your chart and looking at a progressed chart with a knowledgeable astrologer can be both enlightening and inspiring.

But beware of anyone who interprets your chart from less than an evolutionary perspective. People who interpret from a negative bias are, in Miguel Ruiz's terminology, using "black magic." There are several schools of casting a chart. Any can work for you if they feel resonant.

Included below are a few trusted resources to get you started:

Astrology for Yourself. A Workbook for Personal Transformation.
Douglas Bloch and Demetra George

www.moonomens.com
Nina Lekic gives monthly astrological reports from a depth and wisdom tradition perspective.

www.mollymccord.online
Molly McCord offers multiple courses as well as bi-weekly reports in which she guides you in understanding and working with the current positions of the planets in relationship to your own birth chart, as opportunities for your own evolution.

www.thenextstep.uk.com
Pam Gregory's site gives monthly reports promoting a more peaceful planet, as well as offering courses to understand your chart.

www.astro.com
This site offers a variety of free charts. Extended reports are available at a reasonable cost. In addition, it offers many informational articles.

www.forrestastrology.com
Steven Forrest Astrology School
Steven Forrest practices "evolutionary astrology," a perspective that is based on reincarnation, and analyzing the chart from a psychological, spiritual, and archetypal focus.

www.demetra-george.com
Demetra George teaches a form of astrology that was developed and practiced in the late Hellenistic period in and around the Mediterranean, updated for the modern world. She has most extensive descriptions of the asteroids as they relate to our psychology.

www.mymayansign.com
Mayan astrology is a completely different system. It is the astrology of the ancient Mayan culture. Similar to the other forms of astrology, it is based on the time and date of your birth. It differs from Western and Eastern astrology in that each person receives active and receptive signs (symbolized by some aspect of nature such as an animal, plant or star totem) plus an integrative sign for the three different periods of life: youth, adulthood, and maturity. These symbols are described and offer profound insight into our motivations throughout our lives.

Vedic Astrology

Originating in ancient India, uses the sideral rather than the tropical zodiac system of Western astrology. It differs somewhat from western astrology in calculation and interpretation.

Any approach can be valid. Determine what resonates with you.

In Conclusion

Though no system is universally applicable or "true," each offers a contributing perspective into understanding who we are, how we differ from others, and how we relate to others. Any one of these systems can offer insight. Always check with your own internal feelings for a "match." The purpose of the personality tools should not be to label or box you into a "type." And any teacher or guide in a system that pathologizes a student is suspect. If you are drawn to any of these systems, use them as adjuncts in helping you gain greater clarity regarding your natural preferences, tendencies, and opportunities for growth.

On Death and Dying

The Tibetan Book of Living and Dying, Sogyal Rimpoche. A wonderful book, applicable to our lives at whatever stage.

Preparing to Die: Practical Advice and Spiritual Wisdom from the Tibetan Buddhist Tradition, Andrew Holecek.

Reimagining Death: Stories and Practical Wisdom for Home Funerals and Green Burials, Lucinda Herring

A Beginner's Guide to the End: Practical Advice for Living Life and Facing Death, B.J. Miller, M.D., and Shoshana Berger.

Final Rights: Reclaiming the American Way of Death, Joshua Slocum, Lisa Carlson.

Reincarnation and Between Lives

Life After Life, Raymond Moody, Random House, 2001.

Journey of Souls, Michael Newton, Llewellyn Publications, 1994.

Destiny of Souls, Michael Newton, Llewellyn Publications, 2000.

Your Soul's Gift: The Healing Power of the Life You Planned Before You Were Born, Robert Schwartz, 2012.

Light Worker and Star Seed Material

Activating Your 5D Frequency, Judith Corvin-Blackburn, Bear and Company, 2020.

Activate Your Cosmic DNA, Eva Marquez, Bear and Company, 2018, 2022.

Letters to a Starseed, Rebecca Campbell, Hay House, 2021.

Selected Bibliography

Abraham, Lyndi. *A Dictionary of Alchemical Imagery*, Cambridge University Press. 2001.

Aguilar, A. Marina. *Alchemy of the Heart, The Healing Journey from Heartbreak to Wholeness*, Chiron Publications, 2017.

Bethards, Betty. *The Dream Book, Symbols for Self-Understanding*, Element Books, 1995.

Blackie, Sharon. *If Women Rose Rooted, A Life-Changing Journey to Authenticity and Belonging*, September Publishing, 2019.

_____ Hagitude: *Reimagining the Second Half of Life*, New World Library, 2022.

Bloch, Douglas and George, Demetra. *Astrology for Yourself, A Workbook for Personal Transformation*, Ibis Press; Workbook ed. Edition, 2006.

Bolen, Jean Shinoda. *Goddesses in Everywoman, Powerful Archetypes in Women's Lives*, Harper Paperbacks, 2014.

Bolen, Jean Shinoda. *Gods in Everyman, Archetypes that Shape Men's Lives*, Harper Paperbacks, 2014.

Chapman, Gary. *The 5 Love Languages, The Secret to Love that Lasts*, Northfield, 2015.

Corvin-Blackburn, *Empowering the Spirit: A Process to Activate Your Soul Potential*, Healing Concept Publishing, 2006.

Conley, Chip. *Learning to Love Midlife: 12 Reasons Life Gets Better with Age*, Little, Brown Spark, 2024.

Edinger, Edward. *The Anatomy of the Psyche: Alchemical Symbolism in Psychotherapy*, Open Court, 1999.

Fairchild, Alana. *Crystal Masters 333: Initiation with the Divine Power of Heaven and Earth*, Blue Angel, 2014.

_____*Crystal Stars 11:11*, Blue Angel, 2020.

Guiley, Rosemary Ellen. *The Encyclopedia of Dreams, Symbols and Interpretations*, Crossroad, 1993.

Hauck, Dennis William. *The Emerald Tablet, Alchemy for Personal Transformation*, Penguin, 1999.

Hall, Nor. *The Moon and the Virgin, Reflections on the Archetypal Feminine*, HarperPerennial, 1980.

Hillman, James. *The Soul's Code, In Search of Character and Calling*, Ballantine Books; Reprint edition, 2017.

Hollis, James. *Creating a Life; Finding Your Individual Path*, Avery, Reprint edition, 2006.

Hollis, James. *Living an Examined Life, Wisdom for the Second Half of the Journey*, SoundsTrue, 2018.

Hollis, James. *The Middle Passage*, Inner City, 1993.

_____*Finding Meaning in the Second Half of Life: How to Finally, Really Grow Up*, Avery; Reprint Edition, 2006.

_____*What Matters Most, Living a Considered Life*, Avery Reprint edition, 2009.

Johnson, Robert A., *Inner Work: Using Dreams and Active Imagination for Personal Growth*, Harper Collins, 1989.

_____*Owning Your Own Shadow: Understanding the Dark Side of the Psyche*, HarperSanFrancisco, Reprint ed., 1994

Jung, Carl G., *The Archetypes and the Collective Unconscious*, Princeton University Press, 1969.

Jung, Carl G., *Man and His Symbols*, Aldus Books Limited, 5th ptg. Edition, 1971.

Kaya, *Dictionary, Dreams-Signs-Symbols, The Source Code*, Universe/City Mikaël, 2013.

Klossowski de Rola, Stanislas. *Alchemy: The Secret Art*, Bounty Books, 1974.

Moody, Raymond. *Life After Life*, Random House, 25th Anniversary Edition, 2001.

Moore, Thomas. *Care of the Soul*, HarperCollins, 1992.

Murdock, Maureen. *The Heroine's Journey*, Shambhala, 1990.

Murdock, Maureen. *The Heroine's Journey Workbook*, Shambhala, 1998.

Newton, Michael. *Journey of Souls*, Llewellyn Publications, First Edition, 1994.

_____ *Destiny of Souls*, Llewellyn Publications, Subsequent Edition, 2000.

Oliver, Mary. *Felicity*, Penguin Books, 2017.

_____ *New and Selected Poems*, Volume One, Beacon Press, 1992.

Parker, Alice Anne. *Understand Your Dreams*, H. J. Kramer, 1991, 1995.

Perry, Bruce D., and Oprah Winfrey. *What Happened to You?, Conversations on Trauma, Resilience, and Healing*, Flatiron Books, 2021.

Raffa, Jean Benedict. *The Soul's Twins, Emancipate Your Feminine and Masculine Archetypes*, RedFeather, 2020.

Richo, David. *How to Be an Adult in Love*, Shambhala, 2014.

Rimpoche, Sognal. *The Tibetan Book of Living and Dying*, HarperOne, 1994.

Ruiz, Don Miguel. *The Four Agreements: A Practical Guide to Personal Freedom* (A Toltec Wisdom Book), Amber-Allen Publications, 1997.

Sardello, Robert. *Love and the Soul*, North Atlantic Books, 2008.

Schwartz, Robert. *Your Soul's Gift: The Healing Power of the Life You Planned Before You Were Born*, Whispering Wind Press, First Edition, 2012.

Sjöö, Monica and Mor, Barbara. *The Great Cosmic Mother, Rediscovering the Religion of the Earth*, HarperOne, 1987, 1991.

Steindl-Rast, David, and J. M. Noumen. *Gratefulness, The Heart of Prayer: An Approach to a Life of Fullness*, Paulist Press, First Edition, 1984.

Tatar, Maria. *The Heroine with 1001 Faces*, Liveright, 2021.

Twist, Lynne. *The Soul of Money, Transforming Your Relationship with Money and Life,* W.W. Norton & Co., Reprint edition, 2017.

Welwood, John. *Journey of the Heart,* Harper Perennial, 1996.

Welwood, John. *Love and Awakening,* Harper Perennial, 1996.

Whyte, David, *Consolations,* Many Rivers Press, 2020.

_____, *Essentials,* Many Rivers Press, 2021.

_____, *Still Possible,* Many Rivers Press, 2022.

_____, *When the Heart Breaks, A Journey Through Requited & Unrequited Love,* Sounds True, Audio Book, 2013.

Yates Garcia, Amanda. *Initiation: Memoir of a Witch,* Grand Central Publishing, 2019.